Unveiling TB: Understanding, Preventing, and Conquering Tuberculosis

Adinda Nezma Meidina
Yolanda Delia Putri
Akbar Triandra
Muhammad Valdis Muyassar
M. Alif Al Fajri
Dyah Fatha Istiqomah
Nabila Az-zahra Hasibuan
M. Aditya Nugraha
Raisa Qonita
Nafilah Ramadhanti
Putri Salsabillah

Department of Medicine, Faculty of Medicine,
Sriwijaya University

ISBN : 9798303876996

ACKNOWLEDGEMENTS

Praise be to Allah SWT's grace and blessings, which have enabled the author to complete the book titled *"Unveiling TB: Understanding, Preventing, and Conquering Tuberculosis"*. In line with the global effort to eliminate tuberculosis and achieve SDG target 3.3, the author recognizes that knowledge is the key to preventing and addressing infectious diseases. Therefore, this book aims to provide deeper insights into the infectious disease tuberculosis.

We would like to express our gratitude to all those who contributed to the creation of this book. We hope that this book will provide enlightenment and inspire us all to collaborate in the fight to overcome and eradicate tuberculosis.

Finally, we hope that *"Unveiling TB: Understanding, Preventing, and Conquering Tuberculosis"* will offer a greater understanding of tuberculosis and motivate every reader to contribute to global efforts to tackle this disease. Happy reading, and let's work together to unveil TB for a healthier future free from this disease.

Contents

Acknowledgements ii

List of Figures v

List of Tables vi

CHAPTER I. Anatomy and Physiology of the Respiratory System 1

    A. Upper Respiratory System 2

    B. Lower Respiratory System..4

CHAPTER II. Tuberculosis: Definition 11

CHAPTER III. Tuberculosis: Epidemiology 12

CHAPTER IV. Tuberculosis: Etiology................................14

CHAPTER V. Tuberculosis: Risk Factor 18

CHAPTER VI. Tuberculosis: Pathogenesis..........................23

CHAPTER VII. Tuberculosis: Clinical Manifestation 28

CHAPTER VIII. Tuberculosis: Classification and Types of TB Patients 30

    A. Definition of TB Patients......................................31

    B. Classification of TB Patients 33

CHAPTER IX. Tuberculosis: Diagnosis in Adults and Children 42

    A. Diagnosis of Adult Tuberculosis 42

    B. Diagnosis of Tuberculosis in Children 50

CHAPTER X. Tuberculosis: Management 54

    A. Goals and principles of treatment 54

    B. Pharmacological treatment TB 55

    C. Non-pharmacological management 60

D. TB treatment monitoring 60

CHAPTER XI. Tuberculosis: Introduction to Drug-Resistant Tuberculosis **64**

CHAPTER XII. Tuberculosis: Complication **66**

A. Early Complications 66

CHAPTER XIII. Tuberculosis: Tuberculosis Prevention and Education **68**

A. Strategies for Preventing Tuberculosis Transmission 68

B. Public Education and Awareness on Tuberculosis 71

CHAPTER XIV. Tuberculosis: Psychological and Social Aspects of Tuberculosis Patients **76**

A. Stigma and Psychological Impact 76

B. Social Support for Tuberculosis Patient 76

About The Author **80**

LIST OF FIGURES

Figure 1.1. Organs of the respiratory system (anterior view) (Paulsen et al., 2018) 1

Figure 1.2. Upper respiratory system (Tortora & Derickson, 2017) . 2

Figure 1.3. Lower respiratory system (Tortora & Derrickson, 2017) 4

Figure 1.4. Branching of the respiratory tract (Paulsen et al., 2018) . 5

Figure 1.5. Parts of the lungs (pulmo) (Paulsen et al., 2018) 7

Figure 1.6. Microscopic structure of the lungs (pulmo) (Moore et al., 2014) 8

Figure 1.7. Structure of the respiratory membrane in the lung (Hall, 2021) 9

Figure 4.1. Cell wall structure of M.Tb (Jacobo et al., 2023) 15

Figure 4.2. M. Tb specimen on Zn staining (Jawetz et al., 2023) ... 16

Figure 6.1. Pathogenesis of TB (sinigaglia et al., 2020) 24

Figure 6.2. Pathophysiology and transmission of TB (Alsayed et al., 2023) 25

Figure 8.1. Transmitted and acquired drug-resistant TB (Liebenberg et al., 2022) 38

Figure 9.1. The flow of TB and drug-resistant TB diagnosis in Indonesia (Kementerian Kesehatan Republik Indonesia)..........**Error! Bookmark not defined.**

LIST OF TABLES

Table 4.1. Mycobacterium that infects human (Jawetz et al., 2023) 14

Table 8.1. Recommended examination for the diagnosis of extrapulmonary 34

Table 9.1. Interpretation to BTA examination according to the IUATLD scale (Kementerian Kesehatan Republik Indonesia, 2022) 47

Table 10.1. Fixed dose combination based on body weight (Perhimpunan Dokter Paru Indonesia, 2021) 58

Table 10.2. Fixed dose combination in children based on body weight (Perhimpunan Dokter Paru Indonesia, 2021) 59

Table 10.3. TB patient categories (Perhimpunan Dokter Paru Indonesia, 2021) 61

Table 13.1. TPT Regimen Options (Kementerian Kesehatan Republik Indonesia, 2020) 70

CHAPTER I. ANATOMY AND PHYSIOLOGY OF THE RESPIRATORY SYSTEM

Yolanda Delia Putri, Department of Medicine, Faculty of Medicine, Sriwijaya University

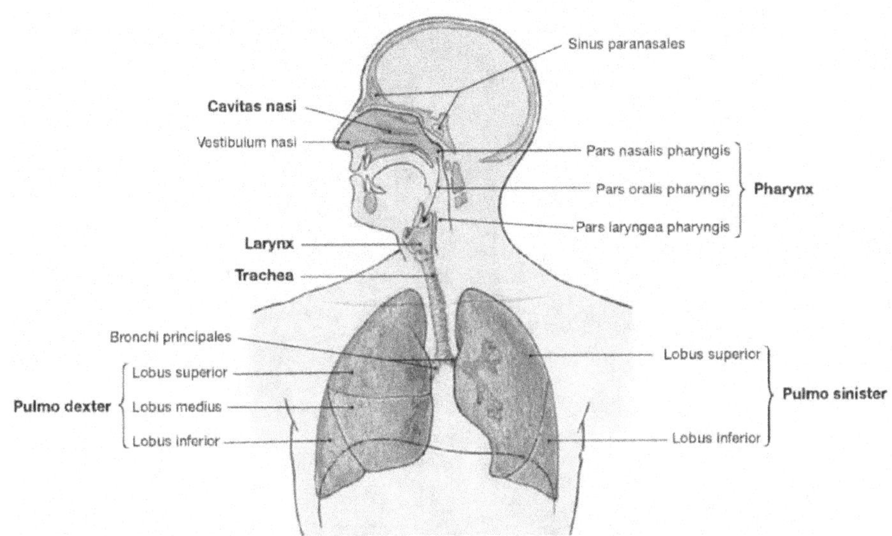

Figure 1.1. Organs of the respiratory system (anterior view) (Paulsen et al., 2018)

The respiratory system plays an important role in the body, namely as a location for the exchange of O_2 and CO_2 gasses, a regulator of blood pH, a supporter of olfactory receptors, and a producer of vocal sounds through the phonation process. The organs that make up the respiratory system consist of the nose, pharynx, larynx, bronchi, and lungs (*pulmo*). These organs can be classified into 2 parts, namely the upper respiratory tract, which includes the nose to the pharynx, and the lower respiratory tract, which includes the larynx, trachea, bronchi, and lungs. In addition, the respiratory system is divided into 2 zones, namely the conduction zone, which filters, adjusts temperature, and delivers air to the lungs, and the respiratory zone, which is the location of gas exchange (Tortora & Derrickson, 2017).

A. Upper Respiratory System

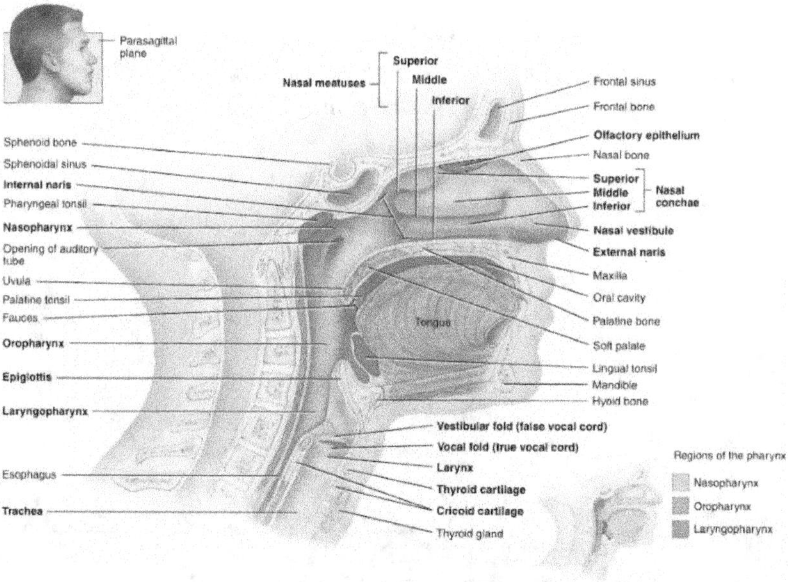

Figure 1.2. Upper respiratory system (Tortora & Derickson, 2017)

Nose

The nose is the opening organ of the respiratory system, consisting of external and internal parts. The external nose is the part that is visible on the face and consists of a framework of bone and hyaline cartilage covered by muscles, skin, and mucous membranes. The interior structure of the external nose has three functions:

a. Warming, humidifying, and filtering incoming air

b. Detecting olfactory stimuli (smell)

c. Modifying sound vibrations as they pass through a large, hollow resonance chamber. Resonance refers to the lengthening, amplifying, or modifying of sound by vibration.

The internal nose (nasal cavity) is a large space in the anterior part of the skull located below the nasal bones and above the oral cavity, lined by muscles and mucous membranes. The nasal cavity is divided into two zones:

a. The respiratory zone, located inferiorly, is lined by respiratory epithelium (pseudostratified ciliated columnar epithelium with many goblet cells).

b. The olfactory zone, located superiorly, plays a role in the function of smell.

As air enters, the air stream is warmed by blood in the capillaries. The mucus produced by the goblet cells humidifies the air and traps dust particles, aided by fluid from the nasolacrimal duct and paranasal sinuses. Then, epithelial cilia propel the mucus and trapped particles toward the pharynx, where they can be swallowed or spat out, clearing the respiratory tract (Tortora & Derrickson, 2017).

Pharynx

The pharynx is a tube located posterior to the nasal and oral cavities, superior to the larynx. With a length of about 13 cm that empties into the internal nares to the cricoid cartilage, which is the most inferior cartilage in the larynx. The pharynx is divided into 3 regions, namely:

a. Nasopharynx: The nasopharynx is located posterior to the nasal cavity and extends to the soft palate. The nasopharynx receives air from the nasal cavity along with dust particles trapped in mucus.

b. Orophaynx: The oropharynx is located posterior to the oral cavity, extending from the soft palate to the hyoid bone. The oropharynx plays a role in the respiratory and digestive systems.

c. Laryngopharynx: The laryngopharynx, or hypopharynx, is the inferior portion of the pharynx that begins at the level of the hyoid bone. It ends at the bifurcation of the esophagus (posterior) and the larynx (anterior). The laryngopharynx serves as a respiratory and digestive tract (Tortora & Derrickson, 2017).

B. Lower Respiratory System

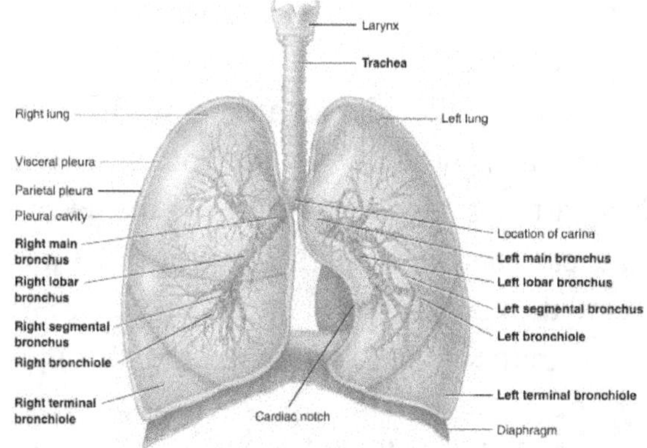

Figure 1.3. Lower respiratory system (Tortora & Derrickson, 2017)

Larynx

The larynx is a tube that connects the laryngopharynx to the trachea, which is located in the 4th to 6th cervical vertebrae (C4-C6). The structure of the larynx consists of nine cartilages, namely three single cartilages (thyroid, epiglottis, and cricoid cartilages) and three paired cartilages (arytenoid, cuneiform, and corniculate cartilages).

The larynx has an important function in sound production, respiratory tract protection, and air purification. Intrinsic muscles and arytenoid cartilages allow changes in position and tension of the vocal folds to produce sound. During the swallowing process, the epiglottis closes the glottis to protect the respiratory tract from the entry of food or liquid. Mucus and cilia in the epithelium also play a role in cleaning the air from foreign particles and maintaining the cleanliness of the respiratory tract (Tortora & Derrickson, 2017).

Trachea

The trachea is a tube-shaped airway about 12 cm long and 2.5 cm in diameter. It is located anterior to the esophagus and extends from the larynx to the superior border of the 5th thoracic vertebra (T5), where it branches into the right and left primary bronchi. The wall of the trachea consists of four layers from the inside out, namely:

a. Mucosa: Consists of pseudostratified ciliated columnar epithelium and a lamina propria containing elastic and reticular fibers. This layer provides protection against dust particles, similar to the mucosa of the nasal cavity and larynx.

b. Submucosa: Consists of areolar connective tissue containing seromucous glands and their ducts.

c. Hyaline cartilage: Consists of 16–20 incomplete C-shaped cartilage rings, stacked on top of each other, connected by dense connective tissue. The open portion of the cartilage rings faces posteriorly toward the esophagus and is lined by a fibromuscular membrane containing tracheal muscles and elastic tissue.

d. Adventitia: A layer of areolar connective tissue that connects the trachea to the surrounding tissues.

The cartilage rings provide semi-rigid support to the trachea to prevent collapse of the tracheal walls, especially during inhalation, thus maintaining the airway open (patency) (Tortora & Derrickson, 2017).

Bronchi

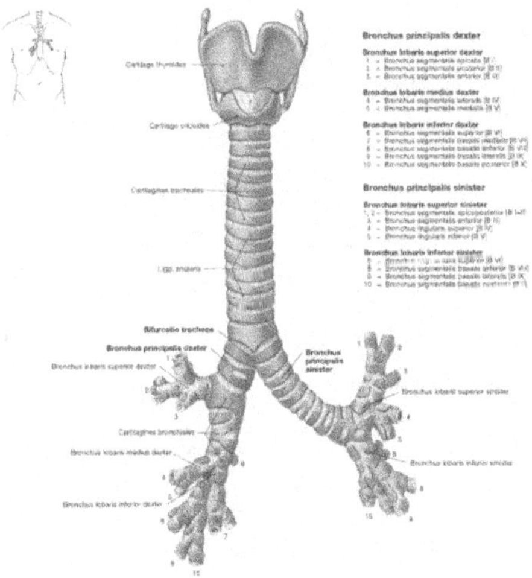

Figure 1.4. Branching of the respiratory tract (Paulsen et al., 2018)

The trachea branches into the right and left bronchi at the superior border of the fifth thoracic vertebra (T5). The right bronchus is more vertical, shorter, and wider than the left, so foreign objects are more often stuck in the right bronchus. Like the trachea, the main bronchi have incomplete cartilaginous rings and are lined with pseudostratified ciliated columnar epithelium. After entering the lungs, the main bronchi branch into lobar (secondary) bronchi, each of which leads to a lobe of the lung (three in the right lung, two in the left lung). The lobar bronchi then branch into segmental (tertiary) bronchi, which include bronchopulmonary segments. From the segmental bronchi, the branches become bronchioles, which then branch into terminal bronchioles. Terminal bronchioles are the end of the respiratory system conduction zone and have club cells (Clara), which function to protect against toxins, produce surfactant, and act as stem cells.

After the terminal bronchioles, the branches become smaller and form the respiratory bronchioles and alveolar ducts, which are part of the respiratory zone. In total, there are about 23 generations of branches from the trachea to the alveolar ducts, known as the bronchial tree. There are anatomical changes along with the bronchial branching, namely:

a. Epithelial changes: from pseudostratified ciliated columnar epithelium in the main, lobar, and segmental bronchi to simple ciliated columnar epithelium with a few goblet cells in the large bronchioles. This epithelium changes to simple ciliated cuboidal epithelium without goblet cells in the small bronchioles and finally to simple non-ciliated cuboidal epithelium in the terminal bronchioles. Particles not trapped in the mucus are removed by macrophages in areas without cilia.

b. Cartilage loss: cartilage rings in the main bronchi are replaced by cartilage plates in the distal branches and eventually disappear in the bronchioles.

c. Smooth muscle gain: As cartilage loss occurs, smooth muscle gain occurs. This muscle helps maintain airway patency, but smooth muscle spasm can lead to airway obstruction, as in an asthma attack (Paulsen et al., 2018).

Lungs (Pulmo)

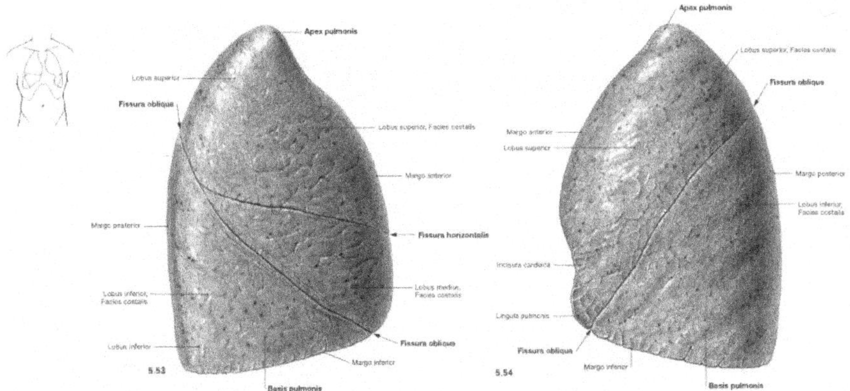

Figure 1.5. Parts of the lungs (pulmo) (Paulsen et al., 2018)

The lungs are located in the thoracic cavity and are separated from each other by the mediastinum. The lungs are covered by a double serous membrane called the pleura, consisting of the parietal pleura (lining the walls of the chest) and the visceral pleura (covering the surface of the lungs). Between the two layers is the pleural cavity, containing a lubricating fluid to reduce friction during breathing (Tortora & Derrickson, 2017).

The lungs have a base, which is a concave inferior part that sits on the diaphragm, and an apex, a slightly projecting superior part above the clavicle. The lungs have two types of surfaces: the costal surface which follows the curve of the ribs, and the mediastinal surface which contains the hilum. The hilum is where the bronchi, blood vessels, lymphatic vessels, and nerves enter and exit, which together form the root of the lung. The left lung has a cardiac notch, making it smaller than the right lung (Tortora & Derrickson, 2017).

The right lung has three lobes: superior, middle, and inferior, which are separated by oblique and horizontal fissures. Meanwhile, the left lung has only two lobes: superior and inferior, separated by an oblique fissure. Each lobe is supplied with air through the lobar bronchus, which branches into segmental bronchi to supply the bronchopulmonary segments. Local abnormalities, such as tumors, can be removed from the bronchopulmonary segments without disturbing the surrounding lung tissue (Tortora & Derrickson, 2017).

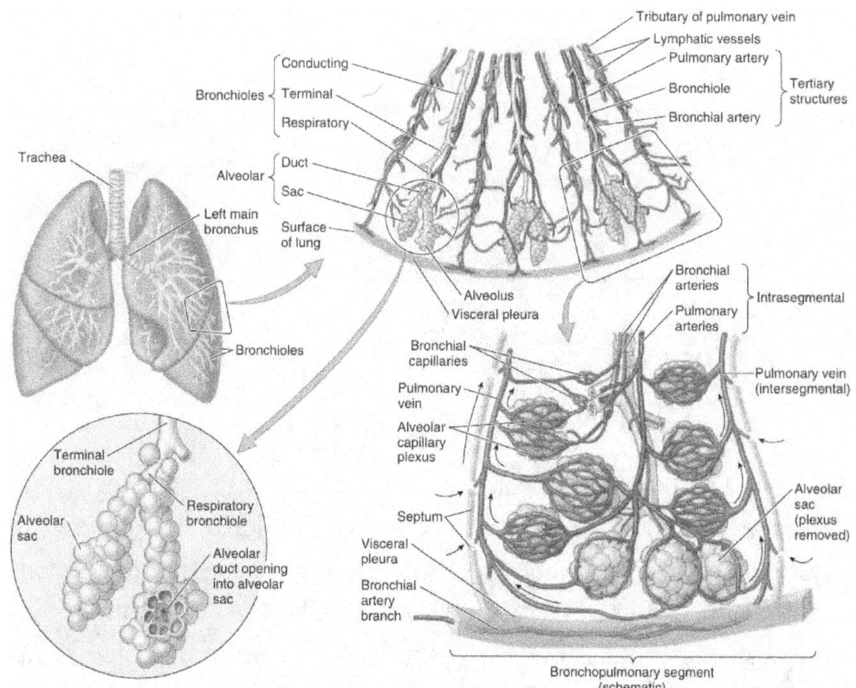

Figure 1.6. Microscopic structure of the lungs (pulmo) (Moore et al., 2014)

Microscopic structure of the lungs, divided as follows (Tortora & Derrickson, 2017):

a. Pulmonary Lobules: Small compartments containing lymphatic vessels, arterioles, venules, and terminal bronchiole branches.

b. Respiratory Bronchioles: Starting from the respiratory zone, with the epithelium changing from simple cuboidal to simple squamous.

c. Alveolar Ducts and Alveoli:

d. Alveoli are sac-like structures where gas exchange occurs, with walls consisting of:

❖ Type I alveolar cells: Squamous cells, the main site of gas exchange.

❖ Type II alveolar cells: Cuboidal cells that produce alveolar fluid and surfactant to prevent alveolar collapse.

Alveoli also contain macrophages to clear particles and fibroblasts that produce elastin fibers.

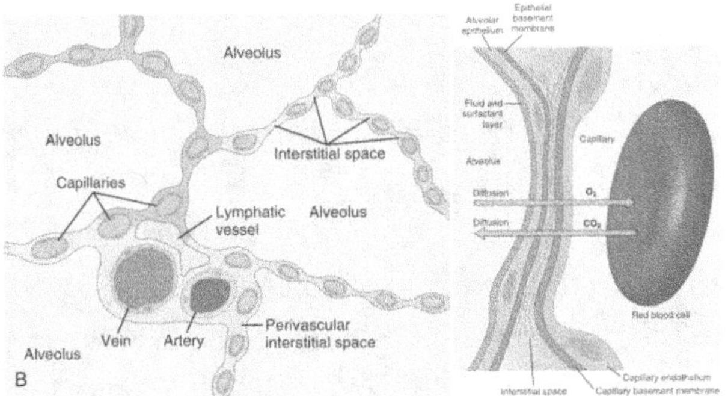

Figure 1.7. Structure of the respiratory membrane in the lung (Hall, 2021)

The respiratory membrane consists of the following layers (Hall, 2021):

a. A layer of fluid containing surfactant, lining the alveoli and reducing the surface tension of the alveolar fluid.
b. The alveolar epithelium consists of thin epithelial cells.
c. The epithelial basement membrane.
d. The thin interstitial space between the alveolar epithelium and the capillary membrane.
e. The capillary basement membrane, which in many places fuses with the alveolar epithelial basement membrane.
f. The capillary endothelial membrane.

These membranes are very thin (0.5 µm) to facilitate gas exchange. The lungs have about 300–500 million alveoli, providing a surface area of about 75 m² for gas diffusion (Tortora & Derrickson, 2017).

The lungs receive their blood supply from two sources. The pulmonary arteries carry deoxygenated blood from the heart to the lungs for oxygenation, while the bronchial arteries carry oxygenated blood from the aorta to the lung tissue. Oxygenated blood returns to the heart via the pulmonary veins. The phenomenon of ventilation-perfusion coupling ensures that blood is directed to the best-ventilated areas of the lung through vasoconstriction triggered by local hypoxia (Tortora & Derrickson, 2017).

References

Hall, J. E. (2021). *Guyton and Hall textbook of medical physiology* (14th ed.). Elsevier.

Moore, K. L., A. M. R. Agur, & Dalley, A. F. (2014). *Essential Clinical Anatomy*. Lippincott Williams & Wilkins.

Paulsen, F., Böckers, T. M., & Jens Waschke. (2018). S*obotta Anatomy Textbook*. Elsevier Health Sciences.

Tortora, G. J., & Derrickson, B. (2017). *Principles of anatomy and physiology* (15th ed.). John Wiley & Sons Australia, Ltd.

CHAPTER II. TUBERCULOSIS: DEFINITION

Akbar Triandra, Department of Medicine, Faculty of Medicine, Sriwijaya University

Tuberculosis (TB) is an infectious disease caused by Mycobacterium tuberculosis (M.Tb). This rod-shaped bacterium is classified as an acid-fast bacillus (AFB) due to its lipid-rich cell wall structure. The majority of M.Tb infections affect the pulmonary parenchyma, known as pulmonary TB. However, in approximately one-third of cases, M.Tb can spread to other organs such as the bones, skin, kidneys, and lymph nodes, a condition referred to as extrapulmonary TB (Fauci, Morens, & Kasper, 2017). Transmission of M.Tb occurs through the inhalation of droplet nuclei, which are exhaled by TB patients during coughing, sneezing, or talking and subsequently inhaled by healthy individuals (Coleman, Martinez, Theron, Wood, & Marais, 2022). This transmission mechanism highlights the critical importance of early detection, effective control measures, and comprehensive prevention strategies in addressing TB as a significant public health concern.

CHAPTER III. TUBERCULOSIS: EPIDEMIOLOGY

Akbar Triandra, Department of medicine, Faculty of Medicine, Sriwijaya University

Tuberculosis is a preventable and treatable disease. Nevertheless, in 2023, it remained the second leading cause of death globally from a single infectious agent, following coronavirus disease (COVID-19), and accounted for nearly twice as many deaths as HIV/AIDS. Annually, more than 10 million people worldwide are infected with TB. The highest risk of developing active TB disease occurs within the first two years after infection, while the risk significantly decreases over time as the immune system in some individuals successfully eliminates the infection. Among the total number of individuals developing TB annually, approximately 88% are adults (with a higher incidence in men compared to women), while only about 12% of cases occur in children aged 0–14 years.

According to the Global Tuberculosis Report 2024, it is estimated that in 2023 there will be 10.8 million confirmed TB cases, 8.2 million of which will be new cases. This is the highest number since WHO began global TB monitoring in 1995, exceeding the pre-COVID baseline. TB deaths were approximately 1.25 million (1.13-1.37 million), including 161,000 HIV-positive patients. The global reduction in deaths caused by TB from 2015 to 2023 was 8.3%, far short of the WHO End TB Strategy's goal of a 50% reduction by 2025. The use of multiple drug regimens that must be taken over the long term remains a challenge for both patients and health systems, particularly in developing countries, where the burden of disease often far exceeds available resources.

By 2023, the highest number of TB cases will occur in Southeast Asia (46%), followed by Africa (23%) and the Western Pacific region (18%). The 8 countries with the highest number of TB cases accounting for two-thirds of all global TB cases are: India (27%), Indonesia (10%), China (7.1%), Philippines (7.0%), Pakistan (5.7%), Nigeria (4.5%), Bangladesh (3.6%) and Congo (3.0%). In the period 2020-2022, the global increase in TB cases is mainly influenced by Indonesia, Myanmar, and the Philippines. Collectively, it is estimated that TB incidence increased by approximately 0.4 million cases in these three countries. This increase is a significant contributor to the global increase in TB cases. In Indonesia alone, there are estimated to be 1,060,000 cases and 134,000 deaths per year by 2022. These numbers are higher than in the previous years.

CHAPTER IV. TUBERCULOSIS: ETIOLOGY

Akbar Triandra, Department of medicine, Faculty of Medicine, Sriwijaya University

In 1882, Robert Koch identified the tubercle bacillus, now known as Mycobacterium tuberculosis (M. Tb), as the main causative agent of tuberculosis (TB). M. Tb, part of the Mycobacterium complex, is the dominant cause of TB in humans and is transmitted through airborne droplets (Alsayed & Gunosewoyo, 2023). Besides M. Tb, several other species such as Mycobacterium bovis, Mycobacterium africanum, and Mycobacterium canettii are also known to potentially cause TB infection. There is no evidence that animals can be a source of direct transmission of M. Tb to humans. However, Mycobacterium bovis can be transmitted through the consumption of contaminated cow's milk. Meanwhile, infections caused by other Mycobacterium species are relatively rare (Jawetz et al., 2023).

Table 4.1. Mycobacterium that infects human (Jawetz et al., 2023)

Species	Reservoir	Common Clinical Manifestations
SPECIES ALWAYS CONCIDERED PATHOGENS		
Mycobacterium tuberculosis	Humans	Pulmonary and disseminated tuberculosis; millions of case annually in the world.
Mycobacterium leprae	Humans	Leprosy
Mycobacterium bovis	Humans, cattle	Tuberculosis-like disease; rare in North America; *M.bovis* is closely related to *M. tuberculosis*
Uncommon to very rare cause of disease		
Mycobacterium africanum	Humans	Pulmonary cultures; resambles *M. Tuberculosis; rare*

M.Tb is rod-shaped, non-sporing, and non-capsule with a size of 1–4 × 0.3–0.6 μm. The Mycobacterium cell wall is a unique characteristic of this bacillus that was first described in 1995. This structure consists of three segments: the plasma membrane, the cell wall core, and the outermost layer. About 60% of the Mycobacterium mass is composed by complex lipids, which gives it extreme hydrophobicity. The cell wall is also composed of mycolic acids interleaved with free lipids that are essential for viability. Teichoic acid, another component of the cell wall, binds to plasma peptidoglycans thus providing high stability and resulting in a compact structure. The outer membrane is also composed of other complex glycolipids, such as trehalose monomikolat, trehalose dimikolat, fosfolipid, glikopeptidolipid, fthiocerol dimycocerosate, fosfatidilinositol mannosides, fthioceroldimycocerosates, lipomannan, lipoarabinomannan, dan sulfolipid (Jacobo et al., 2023).

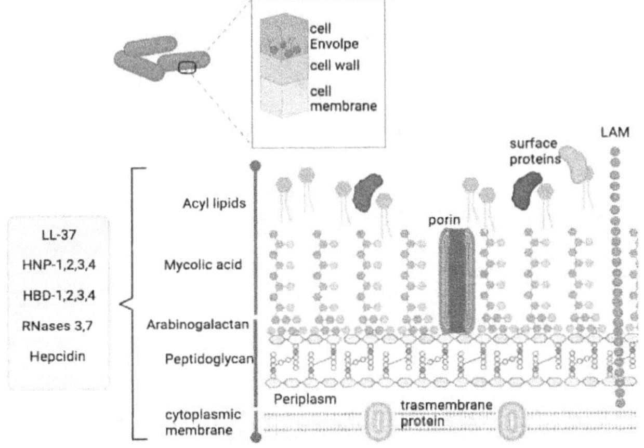

Figure 4.1. Cell wall structure of M.Tb (Jacobo et al., 2023)

The high lipid content in the M. Tb cell wall causes Mycobacterium to poorly absorb common aniline dyes, including those used in Gram staining. As a result, identifying these bacteria requires acid-resistant staining techniques, such as the Ziehl-Neelsen method. Once stained, M. tuberculosis bacilli cannot be decolorized by acidic alcohol, which forms the basis for its classification as AFB. This acid resistance is primarily attributed to the high concentration of mycolic acid—long-chain fatty acids that form strong bonds—along with other lipids in the cell wall. In addition to Mycobacterium, several other microorganisms also exhibit acid-resistant properties, including

Nocardia, Rhodococcus, Gordonia, and Tsukamurella (Fauci et al., 2017).

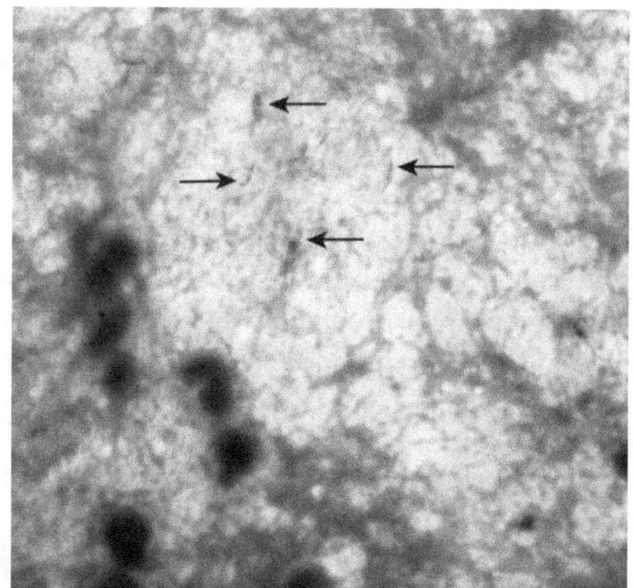

Figure 4.2. M. Tb specimen on Zn staining (Jawetz et al., 2023)

Due to its very small size (<5 μm), the nucleus droplets of M.Tb are able to reach the alveoli space in the lungs, where the bacteria then replicate. Three factors that influence the transmission of M.Tb are (PDPI, 2023):

a. The number of organisms released into the air.
b. The concentration of organisms in the air, which is affected by the volume of the space and ventilation.
c. Duration of exposure to contaminated air.

In the majority of cases, M. Tb can persist in a dormant state for many years without showing clinical symptoms, so individuals can be asymptomatic carriers in the latent phase. However, in about 5-10% of infections, either a further developing primary infection or a reactive latent infection can lead to the onset of an active phase, either in the lungs or in extrapulmonary locations. The risk of developing tuberculosis disease after infection increases in individuals who have predisposing factors, such as immunosuppression, diabetes mellitus, smoking, and malnutrition (Alsayed & Gunosewoyo, 2023).

References

Alsayed, S. S. R., & Gunosewoyo, H. (2023). Tuberculosis: Pathogenesis, current treatment regimens and new drug targets. International *Journal of Molecular Sciences*, 24(6), 5202. https://doi.org/10.3390/ijms24065202.

Coleman, M., Martinez, L., Theron, G., Wood, R., & Marais, B. (2022). Mycobacterium tuberculosis transmission in high-incidence settings—New paradigms and insights. *Pathogens*, 11(11), 1228. https://doi.org/10.3390/pathogens11111228.

Fauci, A. S., Morens, D. M., & Kasper, D. L. (Eds.). (2017). *Harrison's infectious diseases* (3rd ed.). McGraw-Hill Education.

Jacobo-Delgado, Y. M., Rodríguez-Carlos, A., Serrano, C. J., & Rivas-Santiago, B. (2023). Mycobacterium tuberculosis cell-wall and antimicrobial peptides: A mission impossible? *Frontiers in Immunology*, 14, 1194923. https://doi.org/10.3389/fimmu.2023.1194923

Jawetz, E., Melnick, J. L., & Adelberg, M. (2023). *Jawetz, Melnick, & Adelberg's medical microbiology (28th ed.)*. McGraw-Hill Education

Perhimpunan Dokter Paru Indonesia. (2023). *Pedoman diagnosis dan penatalaksanaan tuberkulosis di Indonesia (edisi revisi)*. Perhimpunan Dokter Paru Indonesia.

World Health Organization. (2024). Global tuberculosis report 2024. https://www.who.int/publications/i/item/9789240064670

CHAPTER V. TUBERCULOSIS: RISK FACTOR

Muhammad Valdis Muyassar, Department of medicine, Faculty of Medicine, Sriwijaya University

Some groups of people are at a higher risk of developing Tuberculosis. Recognizing these groups is important for planning preventive measures.

HIV-positive people and other immunocompromising diseases

Patients with immunocompromising diseases are prone to exposure to infectious diseases such as Tuberculosis. One of the most common examples of immunocompromise is HIV (Human Immunodeficiency Virus). HIV infects and destroys the body's immune cells, namely CD4, which causes the immune system to decrease. Decreased body immunity is susceptible to various infectious diseases, including Tuberculosis. HIV can also increase the progression of tuberculosis into disease and increase the recurrence of latent tuberculosis up to 20 times (Udoakang et al., 2023).

People who take immunosuppressant drugs for a long period

Immunosuppressant drugs are a type of drug that works by inhibiting the work of the immune system (Hussain & Khan, 2022). Immunosuppressant drugs are usually used to treat autoimmune diseases such as rheumatoid arthritis, lupus, etc. Patients taking immunosuppressant drugs are susceptible to infectious diseases such as Tuberculosis due to the action of the drug which decreases the immune system's function against diseases. (Bittugondanahalli Prakash et al., 2024).

Smokers

Smoking is one of the factors that can increase a person experiencing Tuberculosis disease. Smoking can increase the risk of Mycobacterium Tuberculosis infection by reducing the work of mucosal cleansing, reducing the phagocytic ability of macrophages, and reducing the body's immune response. Smoking can increase the risk of Tuberculosis disease by 2.5 times (Altet et al., 2022).

High alcohol consumption

Consuming alcohol can significantly impair the body's immunity, and can increase susceptibility to respiratory diseases such as Tuberculosis. Alcohol impairs immunity by interfering with the function of alveolar macrophages, innate immunity in the lung, and the first line of defense against Mycobacterium tuberculosis in the lower respiratory tract (Wigger et al., 2022).

Elderly

Tuberculosis occurs most frequently in the elderly. Elderly with Tuberculosis disease usually have been infected with Mycobacterium Tuberculosis before but the Mycobacterium Tuberculosis is dormant and only activated when they are elderly. In the elderly, there is a degenerative process of both the immune system and organ function so the body is more susceptible to Mycobacterium Tuberculosis infection (Caraux-Paz et al., 2021).

Malnutrition

People who are deficient in both macro and micronutrients are more at risk of developing Tuberculosis because the nutrients needed to metabolize the body's immune cells are lacking. Weak immunity will make the body more susceptible to infectious diseases such as Tuberculosis. The risk of developing Tuberculosis disease increases by 13.8% for every one-unit decrease in BMI (body mass index) (Ockenga et al., 2023).

Having close contact with an infectious person with active Tuberculosis disease

Tuberculosis can be spread through breathing, coughing, sneezing, or talking. If there is one person in the family with active tuberculosis, the whole family, especially those living in the same house, will be suspected of having tuberculosis. Studies show that 63.8% of pulmonary tuberculosis patients are patients who have direct contact with families who have active tuberculosis (Wikurendra et al., 2021).

Health Workers

Health workers have a higher risk than people who do not work in health institutions. Health workers often come into contact with Tuberculosis patients because they work in hospitals. Such frequent contact increases the chance of health workers being infected with Mycobacterium Tuberculosis (Main et al., 2023).

Poverty

A person's income affects the number of Tuberculosis incidents. Heads of households with low income will tend to buy cheap food that lacks nutrition. Lack of nutritional intake will cause the body's immunity to decrease, making the body more susceptible to infectious diseases. In addition, poverty makes it difficult for a person to buy a house and get an inadequate education. Inadequate housing does not have a good ventilation and lighting system, making it easier for Mycobacterium Tuberculosis bacteria to multiply. Meanwhile, lack of education causes a person to not get enough health information such as the importance of washing hands after activities and eating balanced nutritional foods (Wikurendra et al., 2021).

References

Altet, N., Latorre, I., Jiménez-Fuentes, M. Á., Soriano-Arandes, A., Villar-Hernández, R., Milà, C., Rodríguez-Fernández, P., Muriel-Moreno, B., Comella-del-Barrio, P., Godoy, P., Millet, J.-P., de Souza-Galvão, M. L., Jiménez-Ruiz, C. A. & Domínguez, J. (2022). Tobacco Smoking and Second-Hand Smoke Exposure Impact on Tuberkulosis in Children. *Journal of Clinical Medicine,* 11(7), 2000. https://doi.org/10.3390/jcm11072000

Bittugondanahalli Prakash, L. K., Mane, M., Sahu, S., Vimala, L. R., Jha, P., Rebecca, G., Manoharan, A. & Irodi, A. (2024). Pulmonary Tuberkulosis in Immunocompromised Patients: A Review. *Indographics*, 03(02), 054–071. https://doi.org/10.1055/s-0044-1787792

Caraux-Paz, P., Diamantis, S., de Wazières, B. & Gallien, S. (2021). Tuberkulosis in the Elderly. Journal of Clinical Medicine, 10(24). https://doi.org/10.3390/jcm10245888

Hussain, Y. & Khan, H. (2022). Immunosuppressive Drugs. In Encyclopedia of Infection and Immunity (pp. 726–740). *Elsevier*. https://doi.org/10.1016/B978-0-12-818731-9.00068-9

Main, S., Triasih, R., Greig, J., Hidayat, A., Brilliandi, I. B., Khodijah, S., Chan, G., Wilks, N., Parry, A. E., Nababan, B., du Cros, P. & Dwihardiani, B. (2023). The prevalence and risk factors for Tuberkulosis among healthcare workers in Yogyakarta, Indonesia. *PLOS ONE*, 18(5), e0279215. https://doi.org/10.1371/journal.pone.0279215

Ockenga, J., Fuhse, K., Chatterjee, S., Malykh, R., Rippin, H., Pirlich, M., Yedilbayev, A., Wickramasinghe, K. & Barazzoni, R. (2023). Tuberkulosis and malnutrition: The European perspective. *Clinical Nutrition*, 42(4), 486–492. https://doi.org/10.1016/j.clnu.2023.01.016

Udoakang, A. J., Djomkam Zune, A. L., Tapela, K., Nganyewo, N. N., Olisaka, F. N., Anyigba, C. A., Tawiah-Eshun, S., Owusu, I. A., Paemka, L., Awandare, G. A. & Quashie, P. K. (2023). The COVID-19, Tuberkulosis and HIV/AIDS: Ménage à Trois. *Frontiers in Immunology*, 14. https://doi.org/10.3389/fimmu.2023.1104828

Wigger, G. W., Bouton, T. C., Jacobson, K. R., Auld, S. C., Yeligar, S. M. & Staitieh, B. S. (2022). The Impact of Alcohol Use Disorder on Tuberkulosis : A Review of the Epidemiology and Potential Immunologic Mechanisms. *Frontiers in Immunology*, 13. https://doi.org/10.3389/fimmu.2022.864817

Wikurendra, E. A., Nurika, G., Tarigan, Y. G. & Kurnianto, A. A.

(2021). Risk Factors of Pulmonary Tuberkulosis and Countermeasures: A Literature Review. *Open Access Macedonian Journal of Medical Science*s, 9(F), 549–555. https://doi.org/10.3889/oamjms.2021.7287

CHAPTER VI. TUBERCULOSIS: PATHOGENESIS

M. Alif Al Fajri, Department of medicine, Faculty of Medicine, Sriwijaya University

Tuberculosis is a deadly disease transmitted by the bacteria Mycobacterium tuberculosis. Bacteria from the genus Mycobacterium are known as acid-resistant bacteria because they have a complex cell wall structure. Mtb cell walls contain lipids, glycolipids, glycans, nucleic acids, and metabolites that have an important influence on their survival and virulence. One component of the Mtb cell wall has a mechanism to avoid detection of Mtb pathogens, so that the body's immune cell response to Mtb is delayed (Ramon-Luing et al., 2023).

Tuberculosis is a disease that can be transmitted through the air (airborne disease). Droplet nuclei containing Mtb are small, namely <5 μm. These nuclei droplets will be suspended in the air and pollute poorly ventilated rooms. The production of droplet nuclei results from TB patients coughing, sneezing, singing, talking and breathing (Coleman et al., 2022).

When someone interacts near a TB patient, droplet nuclei containing TB bacteria will enter the respiratory tract and reach the respiratory bronchioles and alveoli. The body will respond through the immune system in the form of alveolar macrophages which will phagocyte and digest TB bacteria in the lungs. If the number of TB bacteria is small and the patient has a good immune system, the alveolar macrophages will not have problems phagocytizing and digesting TB bacteria. However, if the number of TB bacteria that enters is very large, it exceeds the ability of alveolar macrophages to phagocytose and digest the bacteria (Alsayed & Gunosewoyo, 2023). TB bacteria can hide and reproduce intracellularly in macrophages. When the macrophage cells die, bacteria will come out of the alveolar macrophages. Alveolar macrophages will inadvertently spread infection to monocytes and interstitial macrophages (Anastasiia Diatlova et al., 2023). The body will respond to this by forming granulomas around the area of infection to prevent the spread of TB bacteria. The lesion resulting from this process is called a primary focus, which is an early sign of TB infection. At this stage, TB bacteria can still survive in the granuloma by blocking phagolysosome fusion and subverting the immune response. In such conditions, infected patients do not show typical clinical symptoms of TB and cannot transmit TB bacteria (Alsayed & Gunosewoyo, 2023).

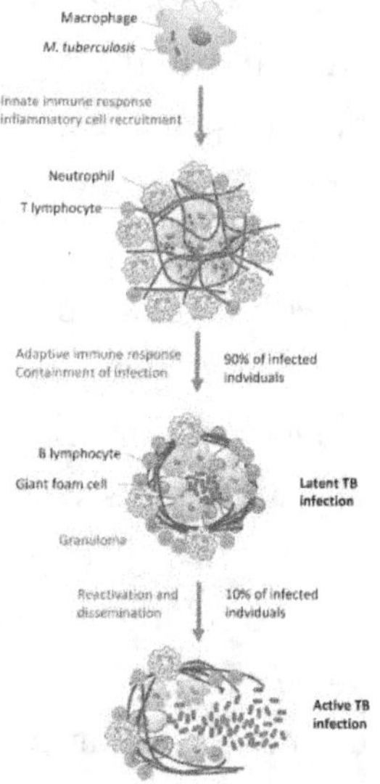

Figure 6.1. Pathogenesis of TB (sinigaglia et al., 2020)

Macrophages can differentiate into foamy macrophages and other morphotypes as the granuloma matures. Foamy macrophages have the appearance of an accumulation of lipid droplets. TB bacteria will disrupt the regulation of the patient's lipid metabolism, causing disturbances in the entry and exit of lipid particles from the serum and their sequestration. The main component of the cell wall of TB bacteria is mycolic acid, which has an important role in the formation of foamy macrophage cells. Both of these will induce the formation of foamy macrophage cells which will later form caseous necrosis in the center of the granuloma. In the final phase, caseous necrosis will soften, causing resuscitation of TB bacteria which will make the patient suffer from active TB. After this, TB bacteria will initiate inflammation of the lymph channels leading to the hilus or what is usually called local lymphangitis. Local lymphangitis will be followed by enlargement of the lymph nodes in the hilum which is usually called regional lymphadenitis. At this stage, the patient will show typical clinical symptoms of TB and can transmit TB bacteria to people around him. Primary focus, local lymphangitis, and regional lymphadenitis are together referred to as the primary complex (Alsayed & Gunosewoyo, 2023).

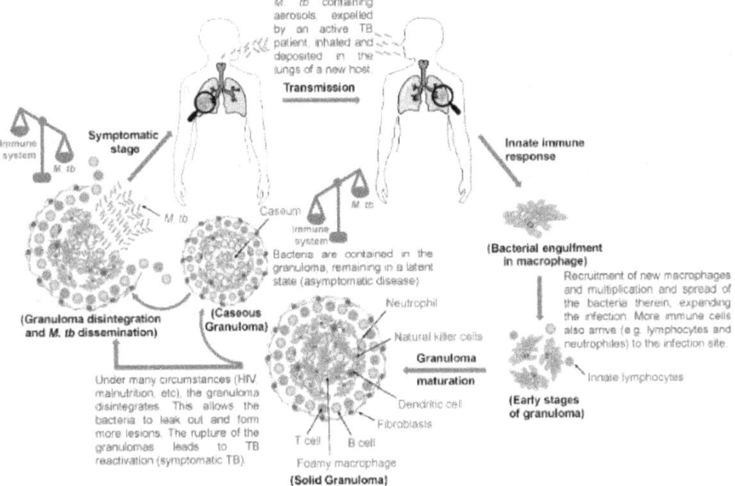

Figure 6.2. Pathophysiology and transmission of TB (Alsayed et al., 2023)

Even though it is synonymous with respiratory disorders, TB can spread and manifest in other organs in the body which is called Extra Pulmonary TB. TB bacteria can spread through hematogenous, lymphogenic and other routes. The spread of TB bacteria is more common hematogenously because endothelial cells make it more likely for TB bacteria to flow efficiently in the tissue. This is what causes extrapulmonary TB to be found more often in the kidneys than in tissues with limited vascularization such as the meninges (Martínez-Zarazúa & Cárdenas-Cuellar, 2023).

In TB lymphadenitis, the spread of bacteria occurs lymphogenously, when bacteria spread from the mediastinum to the cervical lymph nodes. In gastrointestinal TB, bacteria can spread hematogenously, lymphogenously, swallowing sputum containing TB bacteria, digesting products contaminated with Mycobacterium bovis, or direct infection from infected tissue. TB bacteria will enter the submucosa of the intestine and multiply in Peyer's patches. In central nervous system TB, TB bacteria spread to the substance of the brain, meninges and surrounding tissues. Although cases of central nervous system TB are rare, the resulting complications can be fatal if not treated adequately. In musculoskeletal TB, TB bacteria most often attack the bone metaphysis first. This happens because the metaphysis of the bone is the part of the bone that gets the most blood supply so that TB bacteria can more easily migrate through the metaphysis of the bone (Martínez-Zarazúa & Cárdenas-Cuellar, 2023).

References

Alsayed, S. S. R., & Gunosewoyo, H. (2023). Tuberculosis: Pathogenesis, Current Treatment Regimens and New Drug Targets. *International Journal of Molecular Sciences*, 24(6), 5202. https://doi.org/10.3390/ijms24065202

Anastasiia Diatlova, Linkova, N., Lavrova, A., Yulia Zinchenko, Medvedev, D., Alexandr Krasichkov, Polyakova, V., & Piotr Yablonskiy. (2023). Molecular Markers of Early Immune Response in Tuberculosis: Prospects of Application in Predictive Medicine. *International Journal of Molecular Sciences*, 24(17), 13261–13261. https://doi.org/10.3390/ijms241713261

Coleman, M., Martinez, L., Theron, G., Wood, R., & Marais, B. (2022). Mycobacterium tuberculosis Transmission in High-Incidence Settings—New Paradigms and Insights. *Pathogens*, 11(11), 1228. https://doi.org/10.3390/pathogens11111228

Martínez-Zarazúa, C., & Cárdenas-Cuellar, M. J. (2023). Physiopathology of Extrapulmonary Tuberculosis: A Literature Review. *Physiopathology of Extrapulmonary Tuberculosis: A Literature Review*, 11(Fall). https://doi.org/10.15404/msrj/10.2023.254

Ramon-Luing, L. A., Palacios, Y., Ruiz, A., Téllez-Navarrete, N. A., & Chavez-Galan, L. (2023). Virulence Factors of Mycobacterium tuberculosis as Modulators of Cell Death Mechanisms. *Pathogens*, 12(6). 839. https://doi.org/10.3390/pathogens12060839

Sinigaglia, A., Peta, E., Riccetti, S., Venkateswaran, S., Manganelli, R., & Barzon, L. (2020). Tuberculosis-Associated MicroRNAs: From Pathogenesis to Disease Biomarkers. *Cells*, 9(10), 2160. https://doi.org/10.3390/cells9102160

CHAPTER VII. TUBERCULOSIS: CLINICAL MANIFESTATION

Putri Salsabillah, Department of medicine, Faculty of Medicine, Sriwijaya University

Complaints experienced by tuberculosis (TB) patients vary widely. In some cases, pulmonary TB patients may not exhibit any symptoms during a health check. The most common symptoms include:

Fever

Fever is usually mild (subfebrile) and resembles flu symptoms, although in some cases, body temperature can reach 40–41°C. Episodes of fever may subside temporarily but often recur. This recurring pattern makes patients feel as though they never fully recover from flu-like symptoms. The condition is influenced by the patient's immune system and the severity of the tuberculosis infection.

Cough/Coughing Up Blood

This symptom is frequently observed in TB patients. Coughing occurs due to irritation of the bronchi and serves to expel inflammatory products. Symptoms of coughing may only emerge after the disease has progressed in the lung tissue over several weeks or months. Initially, the cough is dry (non-productive), but as inflammation advances, it becomes productive (producing sputum). In severe cases, the cough may be accompanied by blood, caused by ruptured blood vessels most commonly in cavity areas, though it can also occur in bronchial wall ulcers.

Shortness of Breath

This symptom is typically absent in the early stages of the disease. Shortness of breath becomes more evident in advanced TB cases, particularly when infiltration affects half of the lungs or more.

Chest Pain

Chest pain is relatively uncommon but can occur if the inflammation extends to the pleura, resulting in pleurisy. The pain is caused by friction between the pleura during breathing.

Malaise

As a chronic inflammatory disease, TB often leads to symptoms of malaise, such as loss of appetite (anorexia), weight loss, headache, chills, muscle pain, night sweats, and a general feeling of weakness. These symptoms tend to worsen over time and recur intermittently without a consistent pattern (Perhimpunan Dokter Spesialis Penyakit Dalam Indonesia, 2014).

References

Perhimpunan Dokter Spesialis Penyakit Dalam Indonesia (PAPDI). (2014). Tuberkulosis. In *Perhimpunan Dokter Spesialis Penyakit Dalam Indonesia* (Ed.6), Pulmonologi (pp. 2234). Pusat Penerbitan Departemen Ilmu Penyakit Dalam FKUI.

CHAPTER VIII. TUBERCULOSIS: CLASSIFICATION AND TYPES OF TB PATIENTS

Dyah Fatha Istiqomah, Department of medicine, Faculty of Medicine, Sriwijaya University

A TB diagnosis is an effort to establish or determine someone as a TB patient according to the complaints and symptoms of the disease caused by Mycobacterium tuberculosis. TB patients must be distinguished based on the classification and type of their disease for the purpose of treatment and disease surveillance after being diagnosed with TB. Based on (The Indonesian Lung Doctors Association, 2021), this classification is very necessary with the aim of:

a. Improve the quality of accurate patient recording and reporting.
b. Determine the right combination of drugs.
c. Standardize the data collection process for TB prevention and control programs.
d. Facilitate the evaluation of the proportion of cases based on the location of the disease, the results of supporting examinations, and the results of treatment history.
e. Facilitate cohort analysis.
f. Facilitate monitoring of progress and evaluation of the success of TB programs at various levels appropriately both within and between districts, cities, provinces, nationally, and globally.

A presumptive TB patient is someone who has complaints or clinical symptoms that support TB (previously known as suspected TB). The clinical manifestations of TB vary depending on the patient's immune status, route of spread, and affected organs. According to the journal (Mary Lilián Carabalí-Isajar et al., 2023), the typical clinical manifestations found in pulmonary TB usually consist of acute febrile syndrome, non-productive cough, pleuritic chest pain, dyspnea, night sweats, chills, and weight loss. The main symptom of a pulmonary TB patient is a cough with phlegm for 2 weeks or more. Based on (TB CARE I, 2014), all patients, including children, with an unexplained cough that lasts two weeks or more or with other findings on an unexplained chest X-ray that support TB should be evaluated for TB. In HIV-positive patients, in most cases, cough is not a typical symptom of TB, so the cough symptom does not always have to last for 2 weeks or more.

To ensure early diagnosis, health care providers must be aware of the risk factors for tuberculosis (TB) for individuals and groups and perform rapid clinical evaluation and appropriate diagnostic testing for people with symptoms and findings that support TB (TB CARE I, 2014).

A. Definition of TB Patients

The definition of a TB case, as explained by the Indonesian Lung Doctors Association in 2021, includes:

❖ A definitive TB case is a TB patient with Mycobacterium tuberculosis complex identified from clinical specimens (tissue, body fluids, throat swabs, etc.) and culture. In countries with limited laboratory capacity in identifying M. tuberculosis, a case of pulmonary TB can be confirmed if one or more positive BTA sputum is found, or

❖ A patient who, after undergoing supporting examinations for TB, is diagnosed with TB by a doctor or health worker and is treated with a complete combination and duration of treatment.

TB cases are divided into two main classifications (Kementerian Kesehatan Republik Indonesia, 2020). These classifications are:

a. Bacteriologically confirmed TB patients

Bacteriologically confirmed TB patients are TB patients who are proven positive for bacteriology in the results of examinations (examples of bacteriological tests are sputum, body fluids, and tissues) through direct microscopic examination, TCM TB, or culture. Included in this group of patients are:

- ❖ Pulmonary TB patients with positive BTA
- ❖ Pulmonary TB patients with positive M.TB culture results
- ❖ Pulmonary TB patients with positive M.TB rapid test results
- ❖ Extrapulmonary TB patients confirmed bacteriologically, either with BTA, culture, or rapid test from affected tissue samples.
- ❖ Childhood TB diagnosed by bacteriological examination.

b. TB patients are clinically diagnosed

Clinically diagnosed TB patients are patients who do not meet the criteria for bacteriological diagnosis but are diagnosed as active TB patients by a doctor, and it is decided to be given TB treatment.

Included in this group of patients are:

- ❖ Patients with negative BTA pulmonary TB with chest X-ray results supporting TB.
- ❖ Patients with negative BTA pulmonary TB with no clinical improvement after being given non-OAT antibiotics and have risk factors
- ❖ TB Patients with extrapulmonary TB were diagnosed clinically, laboratoryly, and histopathologically without bacteriological confirmation.
- ❖ TB in children diagnosed with a scoring system.

TB patients who are clinically diagnosed and then bacteriologically confirmed positive (either before or after starting treatment) should be reclassified as bacteriologically confirmed TB patients.

TB treatment based on clinical diagnosis is only recommended for patients with the following considerations: (Kementerian Kesehatan Republik Indonesia, 2020)

❖ Complaints, symptoms, and clinical conditions strongly support a TB diagnosis

❖ The patient's condition requires immediate treatment, for example, in cases of TB meningitis, miliary TB, patients with HIV positive, TB pericarditis, and adrenal TB.

This is intended to avoid overdiagnosis and situations that are detrimental to the patient.

B. Classification of TB Patients

Apart from grouping patients according to the definition, the diagnosis of TB with bacteriological or clinical confirmation can be classified based on:

a. Anatomical location of the disease

Pulmonary tuberculosis

Pulmonary tuberculosis (TB) is a case of TB involving the lung parenchyma or tracheobronchial. Miliary TB is classified as pulmonary TB because there are lesions in the lungs. Patients who experience pulmonary and extrapulmonary TB should be classified as pulmonary TB cases (Kementerian Kesehatan Republik Indonesia, 2020).

All patients suspected of having pulmonary TB, including children, must provide at least two sputum specimens (if they are able to produce sputum) for microscopic examination or one sputum specimen for TCM TB MTB/RIF examination in a laboratory that has been tested for quality (TB CARE I, 2014).

Extrapulmonary tuberculosis

Extrapulmonary tuberculosis (TB) is a case of TB diagnosed bacteriologically or clinically involving organs outside the lung parenchyma, such as the pleura, lymph nodes, abdomen, genitourinary tract, skin, bones, joints, and meninges. The most commonly affected joints are weight-bearing joints. Cases of extrapulmonary TB can be confirmed clinically or histologically after maximum efforts have been made with bacteriological confirmation (Kementerian Kesehatan Republik Indonesia, 2020).

Based on the journal (Lakhani et al., 2022), the diagnosis of tuberculosis in patients with extrapulmonary tuberculosis is often missed, which results in a delay in starting appropriate treatment. This is because the existing complaints are generally non-specific or can be said to be non-classical; radiological signs are not well formed in the early stages and gradually develop with further disease progression.

For all patients suspected of having extrapulmonary TB, including children, appropriate specimens from the affected body part should be taken for microbiological and histological examination (TB CARE I, 2014). Details regarding the recommended examinations for the diagnosis of extrapulmonary tuberculosis can be found in Table X below according to the guidelines of the Ministry of Health of the Republic of Indonesia in 2020 (Kementerian Kesehatan Republik Indonesia, 2020).

Table 8.1. Recommended examination for the diagnosis of extrapulmonary

Organ	Imaging	Specimen	Bacteriological/ histopathological examination
Lymph gland	Ultrasonography (USG), computed tomography (CT), magnetic resonance imaging (MRI)	Biopsy at the site of the associated lymph node	Culture/microscopic/TCM/histopathology
Pleura	Plain radiographs and bronchoscopy	Pleura and pleural fluid	Culture/microscopy/ histopathology

Bones or Joints	Plain X-ray, CT, MRI	Location of paraspinal and joint abscess disease	Culture/microscopy/ histopathology
Digestive system	USG, CT abdomen, laparoscopy	Omentum, colon, liver, ascitic fluid, gastric fluid	Culture/ microscopy/ TCM/ histopathology
Genital system, urinary tract	Urography Ultrasonography	Morning urine Endometrial tissue	Culture/microscopy/ histopathology
Central nervous system and meninges	Head CT scan/ MRI with contrast	Tuberculoma Cerebrospinal fluid Culture/TCM/histopathology/cerebrospinal fluid (CSF)	Culture/TCM/ histopathology
Skin		Skin tissue	Culture/ histopathology
Pericardium	Echocardiogram Electrocardiography	Pericardium Pericardial fluid	Culture/ microscopy/ histopathology
Liver abscess	Ultrasonography	Abscess fluid	Culture/ microscopic

b. Previous medical history

Based on (Kementerian Kesehatan Republik Indonesia, 2020), the following is based on treatment history:

New cases

New cases are patients who have never received OAT before or have a history of receiving OAT for less than 1 month (<28 doses if using program drugs).

Case with history of treatment

Cases with a history of treatment are patients who have received OAT for 1 month or more (>28 doses if using program drugs). These cases are further classified based on the results of the last treatment as follows:

❖ Relapse cases are TB patients who have previously received OAT and were declared cured or complete treatment at the end of treatment and are currently diagnosed with a TB episode (either due to reactivation or a new episode due to reinfection).

❖ Cases of treatment after failure are patients who have previously received OAT and were declared to have failed at the end of treatment.

❖ Cases of treatment after discontinuation (loss to follow-up) are patients who have taken OAT for 1 month or more and have not continued it for more than 2 consecutive months and are declared lost to follow-up as a result of treatment.

❖ Other cases are patients who have previously received OAT but the final results of their treatment are unknown or not documented.

Case with an unknown treatment history

Cases with an unknown treatment history are patients whose previous treatment history is unknown and therefore cannot be included in any of the above categories.

There is a risk of drug resistance in patients, so it is important to identify previous treatment history. Resistance of M. tuberculosis bacteria to OAT is a condition when the bacteria can no longer be killed with OAT. Drug-resistant TB (TB-RO) is basically an event caused by its users as a result of inadequate treatment of TB patients or transmission from TB-RO patients.

Before starting treatment, a culture examination and drug sensitivity test should be carried out using the fastest WHO-approved (TCM TB MTB/Rif or LPA (Hain test and genoscholar) for all patients with a history of OAT use. Patients at risk of drug-resistant TB, with HIV, or who are very sick, should be examined with TCM TB MTB/RIF as an initial diagnostic examination (TB CARE I, 2014).

Suspected TB-RO are all people who have TB symptoms with one or more of the following criteria:

❖ TB patients who failed treatment category 2

❖ TB patients who did not convert after 3 months of treatment.

❖ TB patients who have a history of non-standard TB treatment and use quinolones and second-line injection drugs for at least 1 month

❖ TB patients who failed treatment category 1

❖ TB patients who did not convert

❖ TB patients who relapsed (relapsed), category 1 and category 2

❖ TB patients who returned after loss to follow-up (neglected treatment/default)

❖ Suspected TB who has a history of close contact with TB RO patients

❖ TB-HIV co-infected patients who do not respond clinically or bacteriologically to OAT administration (if the initial diagnosis does not use TCM).

As explained based on (Kementerian Kesehatan Republik Indonesia, 2020), patients with one or more of the above criteria are patients at high risk for RO TB and must be immediately followed up with a diagnosis.

Drug-resistant TB can occur through two mechanisms, namely through direct transmission of genetically resistant bacteria (transmitted resistance) or intra-patient resistance evolution (acquired resistance). According to (Liebenberg et al., 2022), the following are the mechanisms of drug-resistant TB.

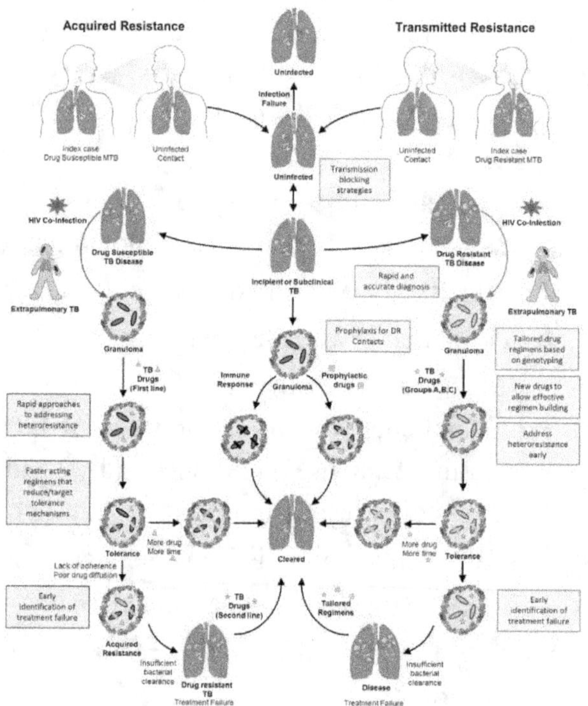

Figure 8.1. Transmitted and acquired drug-resistant TB (Liebenberg et al., 2022)

c. Drug sensitivity test results

    The grouping of patients here is based on the results of the sensitivity test. The results of the sensitivity test aim to determine whether or not there is resistance of M. tuberculosis to OAT and are used to establish a diagnosis of RO TB. Examples of tests from Mycobacterium tuberculosis to OAT, as in (Kementerian Kesehatan Republik Indonesia, 2020) can be:

❖ Monoresistant (TB MR): resistance to one type of first-line OAT.

- ❖ Polyresistant (TB PR): resistance to more than one type of first-line OAT other than isoniazid (H) and rifampicin (R) simultaneously.
- ❖ Multidrug resistant (TB MDR): at least resistant to isoniazid (H) and rifampicin (R) simultaneously.
- ❖ Extensive drug resistant (TB XDR): MDR-TB that is resistant to one of the fluoroquinolone OATs and one of the second-line injectable OATs (kanamycin, capreomycin, and amikacin).
- ❖ Rifampicin resistant (TB RR): proven resistant to Rifampicin using either the genotype method (rapid test) or the phenotype method (conventional), with or without detectable resistance to other OATs. Included in the TB RR group are all forms of TB MR, TB PR, TB MDR, and TB XDR that are proven resistant to rifampicin.

d. HIV status

Tuberculosis in HIV/AIDS patients (TB-HIV) is often found with a prevalence of 29–37 times higher compared to TB without HIV, so all TB patients must know their HIV status in accordance with applicable laws. Patients must sign a refusal letter if they are not willing to be tested for HIV. The following is a classification based on HIV status as explained by the Indonesian Ministry of Health in 2020:

- ❖ TB cases with HIV positive, cases of TB confirmed bacteriologically or diagnosed clinically in patients who have HIV-positive test results, either performed at the time of TB diagnosis or there is evidence that the patient has been registered in the HIV register (pre-ART register or ART register).
- ❖ TB cases with negative HIV, cases of TB confirmed bacteriologically or diagnosed clinically in patients who have negative results for the HIV test performed

at the time of TB diagnosis. If the HIV test results are positive on further examination, the patient must be reclassified as a TB patient with positive HIV.

❖ TB cases with unknown HIV status, bacteriologically confirmed or clinically diagnosed TB cases that do not have HIV test results and do not have documented evidence of being registered in the HIV registry. If during the next examination the patient obtains HIV test results, the patient's classification must be readjusted based on the last HIV test results received by the patient.

Determining and recording HIV status is essential for making treatment decisions, monitoring, and assessing program performance. In the TB treatment card and register, WHO lists the date of HIV testing, when cotrimoxazole prophylaxis therapy was started, and when antiretroviral therapy was started. WHO also recommends TB screening and relevant contact investigations for children and adolescents (WHO, 2022).

HIV counseling and testing should be provided to all patients with or suspected TB unless there has been a confirmed negative test result within the last two months. HIV counseling and testing is recommended in areas with high HIV prevalence because of the close relationship between TB and HIV, an integrated approach to the prevention, diagnosis, and treatment of both TB and HIV infection. HIV testing is essential as part of routine management in areas with high HIV prevalence in the general population, in patients with symptoms and/or signs of HIV-related conditions, and in patients with a history of high risk of HIV exposure (TB CARE I, 2014).

References

Kementerian Kesehatan Republik Indonesia. (2020). *Pedoman Nasional Pelayanan Kedokteran Tata Laksana Tuberkulosis.*

Lakhani, A. F. B., Date, S., Deshpande, S. V., & Balusani, P. (2022). Abnormal Presentation of Extrapulmonary Tuberculosis. *Cureus*. https://doi.org/10.7759/cureus.31390

Liebenberg, D., Gordhan, B. G., & Kana, B. D. (2022). Drug resistant tuberculosis: Implications for transmission, diagnosis, and disease management. *Frontiers in Cellular and Infection Microbiology*, 12. https://doi.org/10.3389/fcimb.2022.943545

Mary Lilián Carabalí-Isajar, Oscar Hernán Rodríguez-Bejarano, Amado, T., Manuel Alfonso Patarroyo, María Alejandra Izquierdo, Juan Ricardo Lutz, & Ocampo, M. (2023). Clinical manifestations and immune response to tuberculosis. World *Journal of Microbiology and Biotechnology*, 39(8). https://doi.org/10.1007/s11274-023-03636-x

Perhimpunan Dokter Paru Indonesia (PDPI) . (2021). *TUBERKULOSIS.* https://bukupdpi.klikpdpi.com/wp-content/uploads/2022/08/BUKU-GUIDELINE-TB-2021.pdf

TB CARE I . (2014). *Intenational Standard for Tuberculosis Care* (3rd ed.).

World Health Organization. (2022). *Consolidated guidelines on tuberculosis Module 5: Management of tuberculosis in children and adolescents.* https://iris.who.int/bitstream/handle/10665/352522/9789240046764-eng.pdf?sequence=1

CHAPTER IX. TUBERCULOSIS: DIAGNOSIS IN ADULTS AND CHILDREN

Nabila Az-zahra Hasibuan, Department of medicine, Faculty of Medicine, Sriwijaya University

Tuberculosis in adults and children is confirmed through the discovery of Mycobacterium tuberculosis germs in bacteriological examinations such as microscopy, culture or MRT. The diagnosis of tuberculosis is generally based on anamnesis of clinical symptoms and contact history, physical examination, bacteriological examination, radiological examination, and other relevant supporting examinations (Isbaniah, 2021).

A. Diagnosis of Adult Tuberculosis

TB Suspects

- **Category 1:** New patients with no history of TB treatment, no history of contact with drug-resistant TB (DR-TB) patients, patients with HIV-negative status, or unknown HIV status.

- **Category 2:** Patients with a history of TB treatment, close contact with DR-TB patients, or patients with HIV-positive status.

Clinical and Bacteriological Examination

1. If **no access to TB Molecular Rapid Test (MRT):**
   - Conduct microscopic examination of acid-resistant bacteria.
     - If the result is negative (-):
       - Perform a thoracic photograph:

- If the photograph supports TB diagnosis, provide a **supportive overview of TB**.
- If not supportive of TB, provide **non-OAT antibiotic therapy**. If there is no clinical improvement, assess other possible causes of the disease.
  - If the result is positive (+):
    - Confirm bacteriologically and begin **first-line TB treatment**. If no clinical improvement is observed, re-evaluate for other possible causes.

2. **If access to TB MRT is available:**
   - Conduct a TB MRT Examination:
     - If the result shows **Positive MTB (Mycobacterium tuberculosis), RIF (Rifampin)-sensitive:**
       - Confirm bacteriologically and initiate **first-line TB treatment**. If there is no improvement, assess other causes.
     - If the result shows **Positive MTB, RIF intermediate:**
       - Repeat the MRT test.
     - If the result shows **Positive MTB, RIF-resistant:**

- Diagnose as **TB RR (Rifampin-Resistant)** and proceed to DR-TB testing, including culture testing and drug sensitivity testing for both first-line and second-line treatments.
  - If the DR-TB testing identifies **TB MDR (Multidrug-Resistant):** Continue DR-TB treatment.
  - If the testing identifies **TB Pre-XDR (Extensively Drug-Resistant):** Follow the guidelines for DR-TB treatment with new regimens.
  - If the testing identifies **TB XDR (Extensively Drug-Resistant):** Follow guidelines for advanced DR-TB treatment.
- If the MRT result is **Negative:**
  - Conduct a thoracic photograph (following the same process as for BTA-negative results).

3. For patients in **Category 2 (with a history of TB treatment or DR-TB contact):**

o Clinical and bacteriological testing, including MRT, is essential for determining the appropriate pathway for diagnosis and treatment.

Anamnesis (Isbaniah, 2021)

Anamnesis aims to explore the typical clinical symptoms of TB patients, which consist of main symptoms and additional symptoms. In patients with TB, the main symptom is a cough with phlegm for more than 14 days with or without blood. Other symptoms that can appear are shortness of breath, weakness, decreased appetite followed by weight loss, night sweats, subfebrile fever and chest pain.

In addition, it is necessary to explore risk factors such as a history of contact with confirmed TB patients, a history of work that is at risk of contact with pulmonary infections, such as health workers, and environmental conditions in densely populated and slum dwellings.

Physical Examination (Isbaniah, 2021)

Physical examination in patients with pulmonary tuberculosis aims to assess the extent of lung structure abnormalities involved. In general, Mycobacterium tuberculosis causes abnormalities in the superior lobe area, especially the apex and posterior segment (S1 and S2), as well as the apex area of the superior lobe apex so that the examination results found can be in the form of bronchial breath sounds, weakened breath sounds, amphoric, fine wet rales, coarse wet rales, signs of pulmonary withdrawal, diaphragm and mediastinum.

Bacteriological examination (Kementerian Kesehatan RI, 2022)

The purpose of bacteriological examination is to help establish the diagnosis through the discovery of Mycobacterium tuberculosis bacteria in sputum, pleural fluid, cerebrospinal fluid, lymph fluid, bronchial lavage, gastric lavage, bronchoalveolar lavage (BAL), urine, feces, and tissue biopsies such as fine needle biopsies.

In cases of pulmonary tuberculosis, the recommended sputum collection is direct or by induction. Sputum collection should be done within one or two days, including early morning (SP), late morning (PS) or late afternoon (SS), with an hour interval between the first and second sputum collection. Sputum is a specimen with infectious properties, so sputum collection should be done away from crowds of people by considering the wind direction when sputum is collected, and should not be done in closed rooms with poor ventilation, such as toilets, workrooms, public spaces, etc. Sputum that qualifies for bacteriological examination of pulmonary tuberculosis is greenish-yellow (mucopurulent) sputum originating from the lower airway, having a volume of 3-5 ml with mucoid viscosity.

- ❖ Ziehl Neelsen Method Staining (Kementerian Kesehatan RI, 2022)

     Mycobacterium tuberculosis has an acid-resistant wall layer (mycolic acid) so that *Carbol Fuchsin* dye can enter the cell wall easily during the heating process. *Ziehl Neelsen* staining aims to test the resistance of the bacterial cell wall to *Carbol Fuchsin* dye despite decolorization using alcohol acid.

     Based on WHO recommendations, the reading of Ziehl Neelsen staining interpretation is done using the IUATLD *(International Union Against Tuberculosis and Lung Disease)* scale:

Table 9.1. Interpretation to BTA examination according to the IUATLD scale (Kementerian Kesehatan Republik Indonesia, 2022)

Number of BTAs Found	Interpretation
No BTA found in 100 field of view	Negative
1-9 BTA in 100 field of view	Write the number of bacilli found
10-99 BTA in 100 field of view	1+
1-10 BTA in 1 visual field	2+
>10 BTA in 1 visual field	3+

TB Bacterial Culture Examination (Isbaniah, 2021)

The gold standard of M. tuberculosis identification is bacterial culture examination which can be done using two types of culture medium, namely:

❖ Solid media (Lowenstein-Jensen)

Lowenstein-Jensen solid medium uses egg-based media to isolate and cultivate Mycobacterium species. Detection of M. tuberculosis on Lowenstein-Jensen solid media has high sensitivity and specificity compared to microscopic detection. This assay can detect 10-1000 mycobacteria/ml within 30-56 days.

❖ Liquid media (Mycobacterium Growth Indicator Tube/MGIT)

Mycobacterium Growth Indicator Tube (MGIT) is a test that uses a fluorescence sensor as an indicator of mycobacterium growth. Mycobacterium will consume oxygen so that the sensor will light up and can be seen using a 365 nm ultraviolet lamp. Positive culture results can be followed by OAT line 1 and 2 resistance testing. Detection of mycobacterium with the MGIT method takes 4 to 53 days with an average of 21.2 days so that this method is simpler, practical, and cost-effective for Mycobacterium tuberculosis culture.

Molecular Rapid Test (MRT) (Isbaniah, 2021)

Rapid molecular testing (MRT) can identify Mycobacterium tuberculosis simultaneously with performing drug susceptibility testing through the detection of genetic material that exhibits resistance. The commonly used MRT test is the GeneXpert MTB/RIF (Rifampicin Susceptibility Test) based on the Cepheid GeneXPert platform with the nucleic acid amplification test (NAAT) method. MRT has several advantages such as high sensitivity of about 99%, results can be known in approximately 2 hours, can determine the results of resistance to rifampicin and low biosafety level.

In addition, another MRT test that can be performed is the genoscholar PZA TB II test based on a linear probe assay to identify the type of mycobacterium and determine pyrazinamide resistance. Approximately 83-93% of PZA resistance is associated with mutations in all parts of the pncA gene encoding the PZAse enzyme, an enzyme that plays a role in converting pyrazinamide prodrug into the active form. Therefore, real-time molecular diagnostic tests such as PCR cannot be used. The linear probe test can detect resistance-causing gene mutations through the binding pattern of DNA amplification products to probes that will cause the DNA strip to change color. The PZA-TB-II test can detect pyrazinamide resistance with 93.2% sensitivity and 91.2% specificity.

The MRT test used to detect Rifampicin and Isoniazid resistance is NTM+MDRTB II which has a sensitivity of 96.5% and specificity of 97.5% for Rifampicin through detection of the rpoB gene. While Isoniazid resistance is detected through the katG gene and the promoter region on inhA with a sensitivity of 94.9% and specificity of 97.6%.

Interferon-Gamma Release Assays (IGRAs)

Interferon-Gamma Release Assays (IGRAs) are tests that measure the body's immune response to M. tuberculosis in cases of latent tuberculosis. When a patient is infected with TB, leukocytes in the form of interferon-gamma (IFN-γ) come into contact with antigens from M. tuberculosis and are then measured using an IGRA kit (Citra, 2020). IGRA interpretation is qualitative in the form of positive, negative, intermediate or borderline and quantitative results in the form of numbers which include antigen, nil and mitogen responses (Isbaniah, 2021).

Radiological examination (Isbaniah, 2021)

A common radiologic examination for pulmonary tuberculosis is a postero-anterior (PA) projection thoracic photograph with multiform features. However, TB disease activity cannot be assessed by radiologic examination.

Radiologic features that are suspected to be active TB lesions are:

a. Cloudy/nodular shadows in the apical and posterior segments of the superior lobe of the lung and the superior segment of the inferior lobe.
b. Cavities, especially more than one surrounded by cloudy or nodular opaque shadows.
c. Shadows of miliary spots.
d. Unilateral or bilateral pleural effusion.

Radiologic features of suspected inactive tuberculosis lesions:

a. Fibrotic
b. Calcification
c. Schwarte or pleural thickening

In conditions of severe lung tissue damage, a pulmonary yield picture can be found consisting of atelectasis, lung parenchymal fibrosis and multicavities.

Other Supporting Examinations (Isbaniah, 2021)

Histopathologic examination of tissues

Tissue histopathology examination is performed using material obtained through biopsy or autopsy in 2 preparations, namely:

a. Fine-needle lymph node aspiration biopsy (BJH)

b. Pleural biopsy using thoracoscopy or Arum Abram, Cope and Veen Silverman
c. Lung tissue biopsy by open lung biopsy, bronchoscopy, or trans thoracal needle aspiration (TTNA)
d. Biopsy or aspiration of organ lesions outside the lung suspected of TB
e. Autopsy

Pleural fluid analysis

In pleural effusion patients with tuberculosis, pleural fluid analysis and pleural fluid Rivalta test show positive results with the impression of exudate containing predominantly lymphocyte cells and low glucose count. In addition, adenosine deaminase (ADA) test can be performed, which is produced by lymphocytes and increased in exudate fluid in patients with pleural effusion with tuberculosis.

Tuberculin test

The tuberculin test is of little value in diagnosing tuberculosis in adults. Interpretation of positive values depends on the patient's medical history based on the size of the induration formed:
a. Induration $\geq$ 5 mm: positive in patients with immunosuppressed conditions such as HIV, patients with a history of close contact with confirmed active TB patients, and patients with typical TB images on thoracic photographs.
b. Induration $\geq$ 10 mm: positive in patients who have a history of contact with high TB prevalence countries in less than 5 years, patients with densely populated environments, and infants.
c. Induration $\geq$ 15 mm: positive in all patients

B. Diagnosis of Tuberculosis in Children

The diagnosis of tuberculosis in children is generally the same as that of adult tuberculosis, namely the discovery of Mycobacterium tuberculosis through bacteriological examination. However, the results of bacteriological examination in children, especially toddlers, are often negative due to sputum that does not meet the qualifications and is paucibacillary (small number of bacteria) so that confirmation of the diagnosis of tuberculosis in children is done with a combination of clinical symptoms, evidence of tuberculosis infection and thorax X-ray examination results (Kementerian Kesehatan Republik Indonesia, 2023).

Anamnesis (Kementerian Kesehatan Republik Indonesia, 2023)

Establishing the diagnosis of pediatric tuberculosis with anamnesis aims to obtain information about systemic symptoms and local symptoms with a persistent duration of more than two weeks even though the patient has received therapy. Systemic symptoms that usually appear in children with TB are weight loss or failure to grow within 1-2 months, persistent or recurrent fever after ruling out other diagnoses, lethargy or malaise that can be seen from children who are less active in activities and night sweats. Other complaints that can appear are cough that does not improve in more than 2 weeks, shortness of breath or hemoptysis especially in adolescents. In addition, it is necessary to further explore the history of contact with confirmed TB patients inside or outside the home.

Physical Examination (Kementerian Kesehatan RI, 2023)

Physical examination of a child suspected of TB includes:
a. Nutritional status of children by measuring weight and length/height. Under-fives need to be evaluated in three months to monitor the child's growth.
b. Check vital signs to see if the child has a fever and shortness of breath.
c. Auscultatory lung examination aims to find any abnormalities such as rales, bronchial breath sounds, wheezing or amphoric.

Supporting examination (Kementerian Kesehatan RI, 2023)

Bacteriological Examination

Bacteriological examination confirms the diagnosis of tuberculosis using specimens collected through sputum, feces, gastric lavage fluid, nasopharyngeal aspirate or alveolar lavage. However, bacteriological examination in children is prone to be negative due to unqualified sputum that is paucibacillary.

a. Molecular rapid test (MRT): MRT examination aims to identify M. tuberculosis within 2 hours and determine the presence of OAT resistance. Currently, MRT is recommended as the primary diagnostic tool for pulmonary and extra-pulmonary tuberculosis.

b. Antigen detection using lateral flow lipoarabinomannan (LF-LAM) urine: This test aims to detect mycobacterium lipoarabinomannan antigens in urine for the purpose of rapid diagnosis in TB patients with HIV. However, antigen detection using LF-LAM is less sensitive and not yet widely available, so it is not recommended for routine TB testing in Indonesia.

c. Microscopic examination of acid-resistant bacteria (BTA) : BTA testing is more recommended for monitoring the response to therapy, but in health facilities with limited facilities it can be used to help confirm the diagnosis of TB. The BTA test is a simple and relatively inexpensive test, but requires a specimen of 5.000 bacilli/ml specimen, making it less sensitive.

d. Culture examination: The gold standard for confirmation of M. tuberculosis is culture examination, which can be performed in conjunction with drug sensitivity testing. Types of culture examination media:

    i. Solid media that takes 4-8 weeks for the results of the culture to be known

    ii. Liquid media that takes 1-2 weeks for the results of the culture to be known, but costs more.

Examination for evidence of Mycobacterium tuberculosis infection

a. Tuberculin skin test: The tuberculin test aims to establish the diagnosis of TB in patients with an unclear history of contact with TB patients. A positive result cannot be the sole indicator of TB infection, while a negative result cannot exclude the diagnosis of TB.

b. IGRA (Interferon Gamma Release Assay): IGRA is a measurement of the immune response in the form of T-cell release of IFN-γ upon contact with M. tuberculosis antigens. However, this test cannot distinguish active tuberculosis from latent tuberculosis infection, so it is not yet popular in tuberculosis testing (Citra, 2020).

Radiology examination

The most common radiologic examination for the diagnosis of pediatric tuberculosis is a thoracic x-ray. However, thorax X-ray images in children are less typical. In children less than 5 years of age, thorax X-rays are performed in the antero-posterior (AP) and lateral positions. In older children, a postero-anterior (PA) thorax X-ray is sufficient.

Histopathologic examination

Histopathologic examination is performed to look for findings such as granulomas with caseous necrosis, datia langhans cells, and/or M. tuberculosis that can corroborate the diagnosis of pediatric tuberculosis.

References

Citra, E. (2020). Interferon Gamma Release Assay sebagai Diagnosis Infeksi Laten Mycobacterium tuberculosis. *Medula*, 10(3).

Isbaniah, F., Burhan, E., Sinaga, B. Y., et al. (2021). Tuberkulosis: *Pedoman Diagnosis dan Penatalaksanaan di Indonesia. Perhimpunan Dokter Paru Indonesia* (PDPI).

Kementerian Kesehatan Republik Indonesia. (2017). *Petunjuk Teknis: Pemeriksaan TB Menggunakan Tes Cepat Molekuler.* Jakarta: Kementerian Kesehatan Republik Indonesia.

Kementerian Kesehatan Republik Indonesia. (2022). *Petunjuk Teknis Pemeriksaan Mikroskopis Tuberkulosis.* Jakarta: Kementerian Kesehatan Republik Indonesia.

Kementerian Kesehatan Republik Indonesia. (2023). *Petunjuk Teknis Tata Laksana Tuberkulosis Anak dan Remaja.* Jakarta: Kementerian Kesehatan Republik Indonesia.

CHAPTER X. TUBERCULOSIS: MANAGEMENT

M. Aditya Nugraha, Department of Medicine, Faculty of Medicine Sriwijaya University

A. Goals and principles of treatment

Generally, the objectives of pulmonary tuberculosis management are as follows:

a. Cure, maintain the quality of life and productivity of patients
b. Prevent death and/or disability due to active TB or subsequent effects
c. Prevent TB recurrence and reduce transmission of TB to others
d. Prevent the occurrence and transmission of TB resistant to anti-tuberculosis drugs (OAT)

While the principle of TB treatment so that the treatment given is adequate must meet the following principles:

a. Treatment should not be given in moneterhapy, at least contains four types of drugs to prevent resistance
b. Given in the right dose according to the indications and conditions of the patient
c. Swallowed regularly and supervised directly by the PMO (drug swallowing supervisor) until the end of the treatment period.
d. Treatment is given in a sufficient period of time divided into the initial stage and the advanced stage to prevent relapse

B. Pharmacological treatment TB

TB therapy regimen

a. Drugs used in the management of TB

In the treatment of drug-sensitive TB (TB-SO), there are several anti-tuberculosis drugs that are often used in Indonesia. The treatment is divided into first-line treatment and second-line treatment. First-line treatment includes isoniazid (H), Rifampicin (R), Pyrazinamide (Z), Ethambutol (E), and streptomycin (S).

Isoniazid

Isoniazid is one of the OATs used in first-line tuberculosis therapy. Isoniazid is also known as isonicotinate hydrazide acid has a bactericidal effect by inhibiting the production of mycolic acid which is important in the formation of Mycobacterium tuberculosis cell walls. Isoniazid has the ability to penetrate into macrophages so that it can kill intracellular and extracellular mycobacteria (Khan et al., 2019).

Isoniazid dose can be given with 5mg/kgBW/day, or the general dose used by adults is around 300 mg given once infection. The dose can be increased to 10 mg/kgBW/day if there are indications of severe infection or malabsorption disorders (Kementerian Kesehatan Republik Indonesia, 2021).

Isoniazid administration is intended to treat tuberculosis infections, both pulmonary and extrapulmonary. Isoniazid is contraindicated for conditions such as Hypersensitivity, Hepatic disorders, G6PD enzyme deficiency, Epilepsy, can provoke seizures.

The side effects of isoniazid administration are usually temporary and low-grade. These side effects can include: Gastrointestinal disorders, Pruritus, and Peripheral neuropathy (Katzung, 2021).

Rifampicin

Rifampicin is a derivative of rifamycin which is naturally synthesized by Amycolaptosis rimfamycinica. Rifampicin binds to the Beta subunit of DNA-dependent RNA polymerase and inhibits RNA synthesis so that it has a bactericidal effect. Rifampicin is also very good at penetrating body tissues and phagocyte cells (Katzung, 2021).

Rifampicin is given orally 600 mg/day (10 mg/kgBW/day) and combined with other anti-tuberculosis drugs.

Administration of rifampicin can cause harmless side effects in the form of urine, sweat, and tears that turn orange. Other side effects include thrombocytopenia and nephritis (Smith et al., 2022)

Pirazinamid

Pyrazinamide is a derivative of pyrazine 2 carboxylic acid that is not soluble in water which is inactive in neutral pH but active in pH 5.5. Pyrazinamide will penetrate macrophage cells and will be active in macrophage lysosomes and form in the eradication of intracellular Mycobacterium (Katzung, 2021).

The dosage of pyrazinamide is around 20-30 mg/KgBW/day or 25 mg/day for adults . In special conditions such as patients undergoing hemodialysis, 25-35 mg/kgBW can be given three times a week (Perhimpunan Dokter Paru Indonesia, 2021)

The administration of pyrazinamide should be considered in patients with liver disorders and hypersensitivity to pyrazinamide. Similar to other OATs, pyrazinamide can cause side effects such as hepatotoxicity, nausea, vomiting, fever, and hyperuricemia (Katzung, 2021).

Etambutol

Ethambutol is a synthetic and hydrophobic compound that works by inhibiting the arabinosyl transferase enzyme which is important in the formation of arabinoglycan polymerization in the formation of cell walls (Katzung, 2021).

Ethambutol is given orally at a dose of 15-20 mg/kgBW/day or 15 kg/day for adults given once a day and combined with other OATs (isoniazid, rifampicin, and pyrazinamide) in the early stages of treatment (Perhimpunan Dokter Paru Indonesia, 2021).

Ethambutol treatment can cause side effects in the form of visual disturbances such as red and green color blindness and decreased vision. However, these disorders are reversible (Swapnali Sabhapandit et al., 2023).

Streptomycin

Streptomycin is a class of aminoglycoside antibiotics that work by inhibiting protein synthesis in mycobacterial ribosomes (Katzung, 2021).

The dosage of streptomycin is 15 mg/kgBW/day or 1 g/day for adults with intramuscular or intravenous injection (Kementrian kesehatan republik indonesia, 2019).

The side effects of streptomycin can be ototoxic and nephrotoxic. So that patients will experience vertigo and hearing loss and can be irreversible. Streptomycin is also contraindicated in myasthenia gravis, impaired kidney function, and the elderly aged > 65 years (Katzung, 2021).

b. TB treatment stages
Adult

In the treatment of new cases of adult pulmonary TB with drug sensitivity, it is recommended to use the standard 2 RHZE/4 RH or if there is no daily dose guide, 2RHZE/4R3H3 can be used with closer monitoring (Kementerian Kesehatan Republik Indonesia, 2019).

In an effort to support compliance and practicality in treatment, a therapy regimen is used where first-line OAT is combined in a fixed dose combination drug (FDC). Similar to the previous standard administration, FDC administration is also divided into two phases, namely the intensive phase consisting of Rifampicin 150 mg, isoniazid 75 mg, pyrazinamide 400 mg, and ethambutol 275 mg and the continuation phase consisting of Rifampicin 150 mg + isoniazid 75 mg given daily. Treatment using a fixed dose combination (FDC) is highly dependent on the patient's weight (Perhimpunan Dokter Paru Indonesia, 2021).

Table 10.1. Fixed dose combination based on body weight (Perhimpunan Dokter Paru Indonesia, 2021)

Weight (kg)	Intensive phase daily with FDC RHZE (150/75/400/275) **For 8 weeks**	Continuation phase daily with FDC RH (150/75) **For 16 weeks**
30-37 kg	2 tab 4FDC	2 tab
38-54 kg	3 tab 4FDC	3 tab
>= 55 kg	4 tab 4FDC	4 tab

Children and adolescent

The principles and objectives of TB treatment in children and adolescents are generally the same as in adults. What needs to be considered in children and adolescents is the dosage of the drug used. In addition, the duration of treatment and dosage are also greatly influenced by the child's weight and age (Kementerian Kesehatan Republik Indonesia, 2023)

The drugs given for drug-sensitive TB in children are INH (H), Rifampicin (R), Pyrazinamide (Z), and Ethambutol (E) which consist of an intensive phase using at least 3 types of drugs (R, H, and Z) for 2 months or added ethambutol in adolescents or severe TB and a continuation phase using 2 types of drugs (R and H) for 4 to 10 months (Kementerian Kesehatan Republik Indonesia, 2023).

In 2022, WHO recommends a short-term SO TB therapy regimen that was previously 6 months to only 4 months with a therapy regimen of 2 RHZ / 2 RH for children aged 3 months-<12 years and 2 HPZM / 2 HPM in adolescents aged >= 12 years (Kementerian Kesehatan Republik Indonesia, 2023).

- ❖ For children 3 months-<12 years
    - ➢ HIV test negative/non-reactive
    - ➢ Non-severe TB based on chest X-ray
    - ➢ TCM or BTA performed with negative results
    - ➢ Mild symptoms
    - ➢ Given by pediatrician
- ❖ For teenagers aged >= 12 years
    - ➢ Age >= 12 years
    - ➢ Body weight >= 40 kg
    - ➢ Can be given to adolescents without or with HIV (CD4 >= 100 cells/mmk)
    - ➢ Given by a pediatrician

Similar to adult therapy, there is a fixed dose combination in children. In children and adolescents weighing > 30 kg, OAT KD is given which is equivalent to adults.

Table 10.2. Fixed dose combination in children based on body weight (Perhimpunan Dokter Paru Indonesia, 2021)

Weight (kg)	Amount of tablet		
	Intensive phase (RHZ(75/50/150)	Intensive phase E 100 mg	Continuation phase RH (75/50)
5-7	1 tab	1 tab	1 tab
8-11	2 tab	2 tab	2 tab
12-16	3 tab	3 tab	3 tab
17-22	4 tab	4 tab	4 tab
23-30	5 tab	5 tab	5 tab

>30	Adult FDC

C. Non-pharmacological management

The relationship between nutritional status and TB infection is a reciprocal relationship where TB infection puts someone at risk of malnutrition and malnutrition puts someone at risk of TB infection. (WHO). Therefore, nutritional intervention is expected to prevent someone from being infected with TB and at the same time help healing in TB patients (Fasil Wagnew et al., 2023).

Provision of macronutrient and micronutrient supplements has been shown to help in the healing process and prevention of complications in TB. Provision of micronutrients such as vitamins A, B complex, vitamin C and vitamin E contribute to helping a strong immune response. (Xiong et al., 2020)

According to the Guidelines for the diagnosis and management of tuberculosis in Indonesia, there are several recommendations for nutritional interventions in TB (Perhimpunan Dokter Paru Indonesia, 2021).

a. Providing food in small portions 6 times a day
b. Drinks and foods high in protein
c. Foods that stimulate appetite
d. Enough intake of vitamin D and calcium by consuming at least 500-750 mL of milk
e. Provision of B6 to prevent side effects of drugs
f. Maintain adequate fluid intake

D. TB treatment monitoring

Treatment response monitoring for pulmonary TB is monitored using clinical, bacteriological, radiological evaluations, and treatment compliance evaluations (Kementerian Kesehatan Republik Indonesia, 2019).

In clinical monitoring, patients will be evaluated every month to see the success of treatment or to see whether or not there are side effects from treatment. Clinical evaluations can be in the form of complaints, weight assessments and physical examinations. Bacteriological monitoring is carried out at the time:

a. Before treatment
b. After the intensive phase (2 months) of treatment
c. 3rd month if after the intensive phase it is still positive
d. End of treatment

If a positive BTA result is obtained in the fifth month or the end of the treatment phase, then the patient is indicated to have failed treatment and needs to be evaluated quickly for the possibility of Multi-drug Tuberculosis (MDR TB). Then for further treatment, it is stated as a patient with the type of "treatment after failure" (Perhimpunan Dokter Paru Indonesia, 2021).

Radiological evaluation is carried out with a chest X-ray of the patient which is carried out before treatment, after the intensive phase, and at the end of treatment (Kementrian Kesehatan Republik Indonesia, 2019).

In patients who are declared cured, an evaluation should also be carried out to see if there is a relapse or recurrence in the patient. This can be done through clinical, bacteriological, and radiological evaluations in the 3rd, 6th, and 2nd months after treatment is completed (Perhimpunan Dokter Paru Indonesia, 2021).

Table 10.3. TB patient categories (Perhimpunan Dokter Paru Indonesia, 2021)

Outcome	Definition
Recovered	TB patients with bacteriological confirmation (+) at the start of treatment and have (-) test results at the end of treatment.
Complete treatment	TB patients who have completed their treatment in full and have no evidence of treatment failure but also do not have negative sputum BTA or culture results at the end of treatment.
Treatment failed	TB patients with positive sputum BTA or culture results in the fifth month or at the end of treatment.
Dead	TB patients who died for any reason before and during TB treatment.

Stop medication	TB patients who do not start treatment after being diagnosed with TB or stop treatment for 2 consecutive months or more.
Not evaluated	Patients who did not have a treatment outcome at the end of the treatment cohort reporting period, including patients who had moved to another health facility and whose treatment outcome was unknown to the referring facility at the end of the treatment cohort reporting period.
Treatment success	Number of cases with cured and complete treatment results.

References

Fasil Wagnew, Gray, D. J., Tsheten Tsheten, Kelly, M., Archie, & Kefyalew Addis Alene. (2023). Effectiveness of nutritional support to improve treatment adherence in patients with tuberculosis: a systematic review. *Nutrition Reviews.* https://doi.org/10.1093/nutrit/nuad120

Katzung, B. G. (2021). *Basic & clinical pharmacology* (15th ed.). Mcgraw-Hill Education.

Kementerian Kesehatan Republik Indonesia. (2019). Pedoman nasional pelayanan kedokteran tata laksana tuberkulosis (Keputusan Menteri Kesehatan Republik Indonesia Nomor HK.01.07/MENKES/755/2019). Kementerian Kesehatan Republik Indonesia.

Kementerian Kesehatan Republik Indonesia. (2023). Petunjuk teknis tata laksana tuberkulosis anak dan remaja (ISBN 978-623-301-427-4). Kementerian Kesehatan RI.

Khan, S. R., Manialawy, Y., & Siraki, A. G. (2019). Isoniazid and host immune system interactions: A proposal for a novel comprehensive mode of action. *British Journal of Pharmacology,* 176(24), 4599–4608. https://doi.org/10.1111/bph.14867

O'Connor, C., & Brady, M. F. (2022, April 8). Isoniazid. PubMed; StatPearls Publishing. https://www.ncbi.nlm.nih.gov/books/NBK557617/

Perhimpunan Dokter Paru Indonesia. (2021). Pedoman diagnosis dan penatalaksanaan tuberkulosis di Indonesia (Edisi Revisi 2). Perhimpunan Dokter Paru Indonesia.

Smith, E. L., Bywater, L., Pellicano, R., Jenkin, G. A., & Korman, T. M. (2022). Acute tubular necrosis and thrombocytopenia associated with rifampin use: Case Report and Review. *Open Forum Infectious Diseases.* https://doi.org/10.1093/ofid/ofac258

Swapnali Sabhapandit, Gella, V., Anumula Shireesha, Thankachan, L., Ismail, M., Rao, R., & Talukdar, R. (2023). Ethambutol optic neuropathy in the extended anti-tubercular therapy regime: A systematic review. *Indian Journal of Ophthalmology*, 71(3), 729–729. https://doi.org/10.4103/ijo.ijo_1920_22

Xiong, K., Wang, J., Zhang, J., Hao, H., Wang, Q., Cai, J., & Ma, A. (2020). Association of Dietary Micronutrient Intake with Pulmonary Tuberculosis Treatment Failure Rate: ACohort Study. *Nutrients*, 12(9), 2491. https://doi.org/10.3390/nu12092491

CHAPTER XI. TUBERCULOSIS: INTRODUCTION TO DRUG-RESISTANT TUBERCULOSIS

Raisa Qonita, Department of Medicine, Faculty of Medicine, Sriwijaya University

Drug resistance arises when TB medications are misused, which can result from incorrect prescriptions by healthcare providers, substandard medication quality, or patients discontinuing treatment prematurely. Multidrug-resistant TB (MDR-TB) occurs when the bacteria responsible for TB become resistant to isoniazid and rifampicin, the two most potent first-line treatments. MDR-TB can still be treated and cured using alternative medications, although these are typically more expensive and have greater side effects. In certain instances, extensively drug-resistant TB (XDR-TB) may develop. This occurs when TB bacteria are resistant to the most effective drugs used in MDR-TB treatment regimens, severely limiting treatment options for patients (WHO, 2024).

In 2023, an estimated 400,000 cases of drug-resistant tuberculosis were reported worldwide, highlighting the staggering scale of this public health crisis. Tragically, approximately 150,000 lives were lost to this disease (WHO, 2022).

According to Indonesian Ministry of Health (2020), the following are the criteria for suspected drug-resistant TB:

a. TB patients who experience treatment failure with Category 2 anti-tuberculosis drugs

b. TB patients undergoing Category 2 anti-tuberculosis drugs treatment but fail to achieve conversion.

c. TB patients with a history of non-standard TB treatment or use of fluoroquinolones and second-line injectable drugs for at least one month.

d. TB patients who fail treatment with Category 1 anti-tuberculosis drugs

e. TB patients receiving Category 1 anti-tuberculosis drugs treatment but fail to achieve conversion.

f. TB patients who relapse after completing treatment with Category 1 or Category 2 anti-tuberculosis drugs

g. TB patients who return after previously discontinuing treatment.

h. Suspected TB patients with a close contact history with drug-resistant TB (DR-TB) patients.

i. TB patients with HIV co-infection who do not show clinical or bacteriological improvement with anti-tuberculosis drugs, especially if the initial TB diagnosis was not made using GeneXpert (TCM).

References

World Health Organization. (2024). *Tuberculosis*. Who.int; World Health Organization: WHO. https://www.who.int/en/news-room/fact-sheets/detail/tuberculosis

World Health Organization.. (2022). 1.3 *Drug-resistant TB*. Who.int; World Health Organization:WHO.https://www.who.int/teams/global-tuberculosis-programme/tb-reports/global-tuberculosis-report-2024/tb-disease-burden/1-3-drug-resistant-tb

World Health Organization. (2022). *WHO consolidated guidelines on tuberculosis*. Module 4. World Health Organization. https://www.who.int/publications/i/item/9789240063129

CHAPTER XII. TUBERCULOSIS: COMPLICATION

Adinda Nezma Meidina, Department of medicine, Faculty of Medicine, Sriwijaya University

If pulmonary tuberculosis is not properly treated, it can lead to various complications, which are classified into early and late complications (Perhimpunan Dokter Spesialis Penyakit Dalam Indonesia, 2014).

A. Early Complications

Early complications include pleurisy, pleural effusion, empyema, laryngitis, ileus, and Poncet's arthropathy.

a. Pleurisy and Pleural Effusion

Pleurisy can occur because Mycobacterium tuberculosis infects the lungs and causes inflammation of the membrane covering the lungs (the pleura). This inflammation results in fluid accumulation around the lungs, known as pleural effusion (Ryan et al., 2017).

b. Empyema

Tuberculous empyema is an exudative pleural effusion caused by hypersensitivity to M. tuberculosis and its antigens. It occurs in 1-4% of individuals with pulmonary tuberculosis (Porcel et al., 2017).

c. Laryngitis

Laryngeal tuberculosis is rare and occurs due to direct spread from the bronchi or through hematogenous dissemination (Zeller et al., 2015).

d. Intestinal Tuberculosis

Ileus can develop as a result of narrowing or adhesions in the intestinal lumen, which is a sign of intestinal TB (Alazar et al., 2022).

e. Poncet's Arthropathy

This condition is a form of reactive arthritis that develops as a result of M. tuberculosis infection in TB patients

(Chakraborty, 2015).

B. Advanced Complications

Advanced complications include airway obstruction, such as Post-Tuberculosis Obstruction Syndrome (PTOS), severe parenchymal damage leading to pulmonary fibrosis, cor pulmonale, amyloidosis, lung carcinoma, and adult respiratory distress syndrome (ARDS), which often occur in miliary TB and TB cavities (Perhimpunan Dokter Spesialis Penyakit Dalam Indonesia, 2014).

References

Alazar Berhe Aregawi, Alemwosen Teklehaimanot Alem, & Girma, A. (2022). A Rare Case of Intestinal Tuberculosis with Chronic Partial Small Bowel Obstruction in a 37-Year-Old Ethiopian Man. *International Medical Case Reports Journal*, Volume 15, 725–733. https://doi.org/10.2147/imcrj.s388269

Chakraborty, P. P. (2015). Poncet's disease: An unusual presentation of tuberculosis in a diabetic lady. *World Journal of Clinical Cases*, 3(4), 385. https://doi.org/10.12998/wjcc.v3.i4.385

Perhimpunan Dokter Spesialis Penyakit Dalam Indonesia (PAPDI). (2014). Tuberkulosis. In *Perhimpunan Dokter Spesialis Penyakit Dalam Indonesia* (Ed.6), Pulmonologi (pp. 2234). Pusat Penerbitan Departemen Ilmu Penyakit Dalam FKUI.

Porcel, J. M. (2017). Persistent benign pleural effusion. *Revista Clínica Española* (English Edition), 217(6), 336–341. https://doi.org/10.1016/j.rceng.2017.05.002

Ryan, H., Yoo, J., & Darsini, P. (2017). Corticosteroids for tuberculous pleurisy. *Cochrane Database of Systematic Reviews*. https://doi.org/10.1002/14651858.cd001876.pub3

Zeller, S., & Ferneini, E. M. (2015). Tuberculosis and Mycobacterial Infections of the Head and Neck. *Elsevier EBooks*, 416–421. https://doi.org/10.1016/b978-0-323-28945-0.00031-4

CHAPTER XIII. TUBERCULOSIS: TUBERCULOSIS PREVENTION AND EDUCATION

Nafilah Ramadhanti, Department of medicine, Faculty of Medicine, Sriwijaya University

A. Strategies for Preventing Tuberculosis Transmission

This strategy aims not only to reduce the incidence of TB but also to create healthy and competitive human resources through a comprehensive approach. This chapter will discuss in detail various steps to prevent TB transmission. At the global level, TB prevention is carried out through three main approaches: Bacillus Calmette-Guérin (BCG) vaccination, tuberculosis preventive therapy (TPT), and control of risk factors contributing to TB transmission.

Bacillus Calmette et Guerin (BCG) Vaccination

The Bacille Calmette-Guerin (BCG) vaccine is administered to protect the body from tuberculosis (TB), especially to prevent severe forms such as TB meningitis, bone TB, or miliary TB (WHO, 2020). Although its effectiveness can vary up to 90%, the vaccine should be given to infants born to mothers with negative HIV status, HIV-positive mothers who have undergone Preventing Mother-to-Child Transmission of HIV (PMTCT), or when HIV status is unknown (Kementerian Kesehatan Republik Indonesia, 2023).

However, the BCG vaccine must be given cautiously to HIV-infected infants due to the risk of disseminated BCG and severe Adverse Events Following Immunization (AEFI) (Kaswandani, 2023). The BCG vaccine is given to infants aged 0-2 months. Booster BCG vaccination can improve specific immune responses such as CD4+, CD8+, NKT, NK, and Th17 (Qu, 2021). However, booster BCG vaccination is not recommended as it has not been shown to provide additional protection, even if the TST or IGRA test results are negative. Additionally, the absence of a BCG vaccination scar after immunization does not indicate insufficient protection against the disease and is not a reason for re-vaccination (Lawrence, 2024).

Tuberculosis Preventive Therapy (TPT)

The purpose of providing TPT is to prevent TB infection in exposed individuals and stop its progression to active TB. TPT is prioritized for patients at high risk of TB, such as people living with HIV (PLHIV), close contacts of pulmonary TB patients, immunocompromised patients, or those living in high-risk environments (WHO, 2020).

The criteria for providing TPT include three main points. First, the patient must be screened to confirm they do not have TB. Second, the patient must not have contraindications to TPT, such as acute or chronic hepatitis, peripheral neuropathy (especially if using isoniazid), or heavy alcohol consumption. Third, the patient must be confirmed to have TB infection through tuberculin skin testing (TST) or IGRA testing (WHO, 2020).

WHO recommends several regimens for tuberculosis preventive therapy (TPT). The 6H regimen (isoniazid for 6 months) is the most commonly used option in high-TB-prevalence countries such as India, Indonesia, Bangladesh, the Philippines, Vietnam, and African countries, as this regimen has proven to be effective, affordable, and accessible (WHO, 2020). In countries with low TB incidence, such as the United States, the 3HP regimen (rifapentine and isoniazid taken weekly for 3 months) is more recommended due to its practicality and higher adherence rates (Lewinsohn, 2016; Yoopetch, 2023). The 3HP regimen is also being introduced in Japan and South Korea, although its use is not as widespread as the 6H regimen (The Japanese Society for Tuberculosis, 2013; Park, 2012). Some countries with higher TB prevalence still use the 9H regimen, which involves daily isoniazid for 9 months for patients at very high risk (WHO, 2020). As a shorter alternative that is safe for patients intolerant to isoniazid, other countries also recommend the 4R regimen, which involves daily rifampicin for 4 months (Matteelli, 2024).

The TPT combinations available in Indonesia currently include several treatment combinations, such as the 6H, 3HP, 3HR (isoniazid and rifampicin daily for 3 months), and 6Lfx+E (levofloxacin and ethambutol daily for 6 months) regimens, given according to target groups as shown in Table 12.1 (Kementerian Kesehatan Republik Indonesia, 2020).

Table 13.1. TPT Regimen Options (Kementerian Kesehatan Republik Indonesia, 2020)

Target Group	TPT Regimen Options			
	3HP	3HR	6H	6Lfx+E
Household contacts < 2 years*		V	V	
Household contacts 2 – 4 years	V			
Household contacts ≥ 5 years	V			
PLHIV < 2 years*		V	V	
PLHIV ≥ 2 years**	V		V	
Other risk groups (age > 2 years)	V			
Household contacts of all ages with rifampicin-resistant TB cases				V

*PLHIV (People Living with HIV); **3HP regimen (rifapentine and isoniazid for 3 months) is recommended for higher adherence and ease of use.

TPT (Tuberculosis Preventive Therapy) should be taken once a day at the same time, whether in the morning, afternoon, evening, or night, on an empty stomach, either 1 hour before a meal or 2 hours after eating. The duration of medication follows the regimen being used, and if the patient is in good condition, the treatment should continue. TPT is discontinued and replaced with anti-tuberculosis medication (OAT) if TB symptoms arise and the diagnosis of TB is confirmed. Medication should still be administered even if the index case passes away, moves, or has a negative sputum smear (Kemenkes RI, 2023).

Control of TB Risk Factors

India, the country with the highest number of TB cases in the world, emphasizes Infection Prevention and Control (IPC) as a key component of the National TB Elimination Program (NTEP). This program is implemented through four main approaches: finding (find), treating (treat), preventing (prevent), and building capacity (build) (Central Tuberculosis Division, 2021). In controlling risk factors, India focuses on improving public nutrition through the Nikshay Poshan Yojana (NPY) program, which provides a direct financial assistance of ₹500 per month to TB patients to support their nutritional needs during treatment (Barve, 2023).

Meanwhile, Indonesia applies the TEMPO strategy for controlling TB risk factors, which stands for TEMukan pasien secepatnya (Find patients quickly), Pisahkan secara aman (Isolate safely), and Obati secara tepat (Treat appropriately). Additionally, isolation of individuals showing signs and symptoms of TB or those diagnosed with TB is practiced to prevent further transmission (Kemenkes, 2023). Adopting a healthy lifestyle, such as avoiding smoking, consuming balanced nutritious food, ensuring good ventilation and lighting in living spaces, and practicing proper coughing etiquette, is essential in controlling TB risk factors (Kementerian Kesehatan Republik Indonesia, 2020).

B. Public Education and Awareness on Tuberculosis

One of the main challenges in controlling TB transmission is the lack of public understanding about risk factors, symptoms, and the importance of proper treatment. Therefore, community education programs become a key step in encouraging preventive actions to break the chain of TB transmission.

End TB Strategy

The End TB Strategy is a global initiative launched by the WHO in 2014, aiming to end the TB epidemic by 2035. The strategy seeks to reduce TB incidence by 90% and TB-related deaths by 95% compared to 2015 levels by 2030. It is based on three main pillars: the first focuses on patient-centered integrated care and prevention, which includes improving access to quality diagnosis and treatment, as well as prevention through vaccination and prophylactic treatment. The second pillar emphasizes strengthening policies and support systems, such as enhancing healthcare systems and promoting cross-sector collaboration. The third pillar is research and innovation, which includes the development of new drugs, vaccines, and diagnostic technologies. The success of this strategy requires global commitment, technological innovation, and community-based approaches to ensure equitable access to healthcare services (WHO, 2022).

National Tuberculosis Elimination Programme (NTEP)

The National Tuberculosis Elimination Programme (NTEP) is a public health program in India that aims to detect, treat, and prevent TB, with a target to reduce TB incidence to below 44 per 100,000 population by 2025. NTEP includes early detection through Active Case Finding (ACF), nutritional support for patients through the Nikshay Poshan Yojana, and the management of latent TB infection (TBI) using Tuberculosis Preventive Therapy (TPT). The Nikshay Ecosystem digital platform monitors cases in real-time and facilitates private sector collaboration through the Public-Private Mix (PPM). The program also focuses on contact tracing, the treatment of drug-resistant TB, and TB-HIV collaboration, with the integrated approach of Detect-Treat-Prevent-Build to achieve TB elimination by 2025. Despite these initiatives, India faces one of the highest rates of drug-resistant TB globally, which is more difficult and costly to treat. Additionally, nearly 50% of TB patients in India visit private healthcare providers.

Strategi Nasional Penanggulangan Tuberkulosis and TOSS TB

The National Tuberculosis Control Strategy in Indonesia is an integrated and comprehensive effort designed by the government to address the TB problem. The strategy aims to reduce TB incidence, decrease TB-related deaths, and prevent transmission and drug resistance (MDR-TB and XDR-TB). The Tuberculosis Control Strategy in Indonesia for 2020-2024 is implemented through six strategies (Kemenkes RI, 2023):

a. Strengthening the commitment and leadership of the central, provincial, and district/city governments to accelerate TB elimination by 2030.
b. Improving access to quality and patient-centered TB services.
c. Optimizing promotion, prevention, TB preventive treatment, and infection control.
d. Utilizing research and technology for screening, diagnosis, and management of TB.
e. Enhancing the role of communities, partners, and other sectors in TB elimination.
f. Strengthening program management through health system strengthening.

Indonesia implements two main programs: TOSS TB and STOP TB Partnership Indonesia. TOSS TB (Find, Treat, Until Cured Tuberculosis) is a program launched by the Indonesian Ministry of Health to accelerate TB control in the country. This program aims to improve active TB case detection and ensure effective treatment until patients are cured. TOSS TB also involves public education and awareness to reduce the stigma surrounding TB patients and highlight the importance of completing treatment to prevent further transmission (TB Indonesia, 2024).

References

Barve, S., Gore, M., Datir, D., & Patil, R. (2023). A study about awareness and utilization of "Nikshay Poshan Yojana" benefits in selected tuberculosis units in Pune district, India. *Indian Journal of Tuberculosis.* https://doi.org/10.1016/j.ijtb.2023.12.004

Central Tuberculosis Division. (2021). Guidelines – Central Tuberculosis Division. *National Tuberculosis Elimination Programme*. https://tbcindia.mohfw.gov.in/guidelines/

Kaswandani, N. (2023). BCG in special conditions. In *Proceeding Book Childhood Immunization Update 2023*. Badan Penerbit Ikatan Dokter Anak Indonesia.

Kemenkes RI. (2020). Lembar balik terapi pencegahan tuberkulosis. *TBC Indonesia*. https://www.tbindonesia.or.id/wp-content/uploads/2020/10/Lembar-Balik-Pemberian-Terapi-Pencegahan-Tuberkulosis_Fix_convert.pdf

Kemenkes RI. (2023). Lembar balik TOSS TB. *TBC Indonesia*. https://tbindonesia.or.id/pustaka_tbc/lempar-balik-toss-tb/

Kemenkes RI. (2023). Petunjuk teknis tata laksana tuberkulosis anak dan remaja 2023. *TBC Indonesia*. https://tbindonesia.or.id/pustaka_tbc/petunjuk-teknis-tata-laksana-tuberkulosis-anak-dan-remaja/

Kemenkes, RI. (2023). Revisi strategi nasional penanggulangan tuberkulosis di Indonesia 2020-2024 dan rencana interim 2025-2026. Pertemuan Konsolidasi Nasional Penyusunan STRANAS TB.

Lawrence, A. (2024). Bacillus Calmette-Guérin (BCG) revaccination and protection against tuberculosis: *A systematic review*. *Cureus*, 16(3). https://doi.org/10.7759/cureus.56643

Lewinsohn, D. M., et al. (2016). Official American Thoracic Society/Infectious Diseases Society of America/Centers for Disease Control and Prevention clinical practice guidelines: Diagnosis of tuberculosis in adults and children. *Clinical Infectious Diseases*, 64(2), e1–e33. https://doi.org/10.1093/cid/ciw694

Matteelli, A., Mkrtchyan, Z., Masini, T., Hovhannesyan, A., Kuchukhidze, G., Ahmedov, S., Kerndt, P., Rossi, L., Yedilbayev, A., Falzon, D., & Dadu, A. (2024). TB prevention activities in the WHO European Region. *IJTLD open*, 1(8), 349–354. https://doi.org/10.5588/ijtldopen.24.0350

Park, J. S. (2012). Korean guidelines for the treatment of tuberculosis. *The Korean Journal of Medicine*, 82(3), 269-273.

Qu, M., Zhou, X., & Li, H. (2021). BCG vaccination strategies against tuberculosis: Updates and perspectives. *Human Vaccines & Immunotherapeutics*, 17(12), 5284–5295. https://doi.org/10.1080/21645515.2021.2007711

Suseela, R. P., & Shannawaz, M. (2023). Engaging the Private Health Service Delivery Sector for TB Care in India-Miles to Go!. *Tropical medicine and infectious disease*, 8(5), 265. https://doi.org/10.3390/tropicalmed8050265

TB Indonesia. (2024). Seputar TOSS TBC. *TB Indonesia*. https://www.tbindonesia.or.id/?page_id=201

The Japanese Society for Tuberculosis. (2013). Guidelines for treatment of latent tuberculosis infection. *Kekkaku*, 88(5), 497-512. https://www.kekkaku.gr.jp/pub/Vol.88(2013)/Vol88_No5/Vol88No5P497-512.pdf

World Health Organization. (2020). WHO Operational Handbook on Tuberculosis. Module 1: Prevention-Tuberculosis Preventive Treatment. World Health Organization.

World Health Organization. (2022). Implementing the End TB Strategy: The Essentials. World Health Organization.

Yoopetch, P., et al. (2023). Efficacy of anti-tuberculosis drugs for the treatment of latent tuberculosis infection: A systematic review and network meta-analysis. *Scientific Reports*, 13(1). https://doi.org/10.1038/s41598-023-43310-8

CHAPTER XIV. TUBERCULOSIS: PSYCHOLOGICAL AND SOCIAL ASPECTS OF TUBERCULOSIS PATIENTS

Nafilah Ramadhanti, Department of medicine, Faculty of Medicine, Sriwijaya University

A. Stigma and Psychological Impact

Stigma against tuberculosis (TB) patients is one of the challenges in controlling the disease in Indonesia. TB patients often face discrimination in social and workplace environments due to the belief that their illness is caused by bad habits or that it is highly contagious. This stigma hinders early detection and treatment, as patients tend to conceal their condition (Lolong, 2021). The End TB Strategy highlights the importance of a human rights-based approach, public education, and community involvement to reduce stigma and improve access to healthcare services (WHO, 2020).

The approaches to reducing stigma against TB patients involve several strategic measures. Public education campaigns are conducted to spread accurate information about TB, including its causes, transmission, and the importance of treatment, which helps reduce misunderstandings and prejudice. Patients are empowered through psychosocial support, such as counseling and support groups, to help them feel more confident in facing discrimination. A human rights-based approach is also emphasized to ensure equal access to healthcare services. Additionally, community involvement in awareness campaigns fosters a more inclusive environment that supports TB patients (Kemenkes RI, 2023).

B. Social Support for Tuberculosis Patient

Treatment Support

The WHO recommends the Directly Observed Treatment, Short-Course (DOTS) program as part of treatment support, which has been implemented in many countries. Healthcare workers or caregivers ensure that TB patients take their medication as scheduled to prevent drug resistance (Burzynski, 2022).

In addition to DOTS, there is also a method called Video Directly Observed Treatment (vDOT). vDOT is a digital variation of DOTS, where patients send videos or recordings of themselves taking medication, enabling remote monitoring using technology. This is particularly useful in areas with limited access to healthcare services or during a pandemic (Mangan, 2023). vDOT is considered more effective in improving medication adherence and reducing negative stigma among TB patients (Kara, 2022).

However, both DOTS and vDOT still leave room for patients to not adhere to their medication regimen. Researchers have thus proposed an innovation called Wirelessly Observed Therapy (WOT), which uses ingestible sensors, wearable patches, and mobile devices. WOT has a detection accuracy of 99.3% and is more effective than DOTS in supporting medication adherence. Patients also do not need to record videos or visit healthcare facilities with this WOT system (Brown, 2019).

TB Survivor Communities

TB survivor communities, such as TB Champions in India, TB Ambassadors in Kenya, and the Treatment Action Campaign (TAC) in South Africa, are specialized programs aimed at supporting TB elimination through advocacy, stigma reduction, and community empowerment. They play a key role in connecting with TB patients, disseminating education, improving medication adherence, and reducing stigma (Yadav, 2022; Mabalene, 2024). Their personal experiences in fighting TB are crucial in supporting patients, voicing their needs, and improving treatment success.

References

Browne, S. H., Umlauf, A., Tucker, A. J., Low, J., Moser, K., Gonzalez Garcia, J., Peloquin, C. A., Blaschke, T., Vaida, F., & Benson, C. A. (2019). Wirelessly observed therapy compared to directly observed therapy to confirm and support tuberculosis treatment adherence: A randomized controlled trial. *PLOS*

Medicine, *16*(10), e1002891. https://doi.org/10.1371/journal.pmed.1002891

Burzynski, J., Mangan, J. M., Lam, C. K., Macaraig, M., Salerno, M. M., deCastro, B. R., Goswami, N. D., Lin, C. Y., Schluger, N. W., Vernon, A., & eDOT Study Team. (2022). In-person vs electronic directly observed therapy for tuberculosis treatment adherence: A randomized noninferiority trial. *JAMA Network Open,* *5*(1), e2144210–e2144210. https://doi.org/10.1001/jamanetworkopen.2021.44210

Fuady, A., Arifin, B., Yunita, F., Rauf, S., Fitriangga, A., Sugiharto, A., Yani, F. F., Nasution, H. S., Gede, I. W., Mansyur, M., & Wingfield, T. (2023). Stigma towards people with tuberculosis: A cross-cultural adaptation and validation of a scale in Indonesia. *BMC Psychology,* *11*(1). https://doi.org/10.1186/s40359-023-01161-y

Kara, G. C., & Yalcin, B. M. (2022). Comparison of in-person vs. video directly observed therapy (VDOT) on stigma levels in tuberculosis patients. *Journal of the American Board of Family Medicine: JABFM.* https://doi.org/10.3122/jabfm.2022.AP.210514

Kemenkes, RI. (2023). *Revisi strategi nasional penanggulangan tuberkulosis di Indonesia 2020-2024 dan rencana interim 2025-2026.* Pertemuan Konsolidasi Nasional Penyusunan STRANAS TB.

Lolong, D. B., Tobing, K. L., Perwitasari, D., Pangaribuan, L., Tejayanti, T., & S, O. S. (2021). Knowledge and perceived stigma towards tuberculosis among tuberculosis suspects by gender in the community in Indonesia. *Indian Journal of Public Health Research & Development,* *12*(3), 16116. https://doi.org/10.37506/ijphrd.v12i3.16116

Mabalane, M., Ndhlovu, T. M., Moyo, C., Moyo, S., & Tshuma, N. (2024). Shifting TB Ambassador paradigm: From celebrity to activist for sustainable advocacy. https://doi.org/10.13140/RG.2.2.36744.84488

Mangan, J. M. (2023). Recommendations for use of video directly observed therapy during tuberculosis treatment — United States, 2023. *MMWR. Morbidity and Mortality Weekly Report, 72*(12). https://doi.org/10.15585/mmwr.mm7212a4

Menteri Kesehatan Republik Indonesia. (2016). *Peraturan Menteri Kesehatan Republik Indonesia Nomor 67 Tahun 2016 Tentang Penanggulangan Tuberkulosis.* Kemenkes Indonesia. https://peraturan.bpk.go.id/Details/114486/permenkes-no-67-tahun-2016

World Health Organization. (2020). *WHO Operational Handbook on Tuberculosis. Module 1: Prevention-Tuberculosis Preventive Treatment.* World Health Organization.

Yadav, S. (2022). TB Champions- An important initiative in the direction of TB elimination from India. *IP Indian Journal of Immunology and Respiratory Medicine, 7*(3), 99–100. https://doi.org/10.18231/j.ijirm.2022.023

ABOUT THE AUTHOR

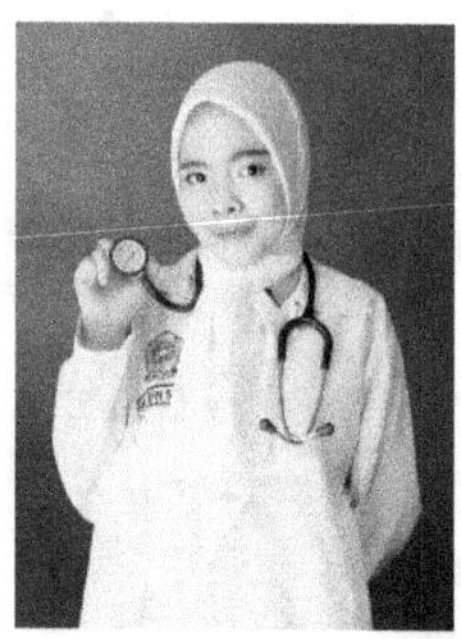

Adinda Nezma Meidina, the main author of this book, was born in Jambi on May 17, 2004. She is an active figure in research and writing as a medical student at the Faculty of Medicine, Sriwijaya University. She has won three gold medals in international innovation competitions and has achieved several accolades at the national level in scientific writing. Currently, she serves as a member of the Core Management Board of the BAPIN-ISMKI organization, a scientific institution that oversees all medical faculty scientific institutions across Indonesia. She has three journal publications as the lead author and two books indexed under her main author ISBN. Additionally, she is involved in humanitarian activities, including coordinating a free health check-up event in South Sumatra, which attracted more than 600 participants. Due to her achievements, she was honored with the Outstanding Youth of South Sumatra Province Award in 2024.

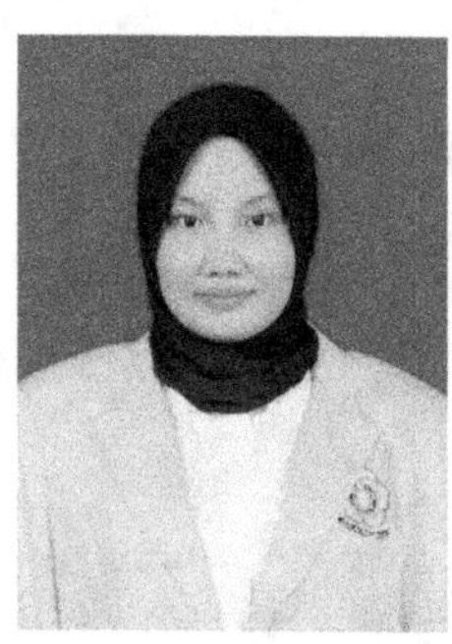

Yolanda Delia Putri, is a medical student at the Faculty of Medicine, Sriwijaya University who is active in academic and organizational activities within the faculty. Since 2023, she has been a member of the Sriwijaya Medical Assistance Team (TBMS) and has been actively involved in various work programs that focus on community service, such as TBMS Peduli Akbar and Community Development 2024. Through organizational education and training, she has acquired various medical skills such as emergency management, resuscitation, intubation, circumcision, among others. In addition, together with her team, she won a gold medal in an international competition with the theme of innovation in the field of medicine, which aims to improve the quality of public health.

Akbar Triandra, is a student who is actively involved in various student activities, both academic and non-academic. He demonstrates a strong dedication to self-development by participating in scientific competitions and producing several written works. Additionally, Akbar is engaged in community development activities, where he contributes by implementing programs that have a positive impact on the local environment, using his knowledge to create relevant and practical solutions.

Muhammad Valdis Muyassar, a student of FK UNSRI who has the ambition to change the education system in Indonesia. His experience in writing scientific papers, participating in olympiads, and seeking scholarships since high school reflects his dedication in achieving higher education. The density of medical studies did not prevent him from being active in organizations. By participating in the Sriwijaya Medical Assistance Team organization, FK UNSRI also shows his commitment to serving the community. In addition, his interest in writing books reflects his intention to share knowledge through the medium of writing.

M. Alif Al Fajri, who serves as the Head of the Department of Strategic Studies and Action of BEM KM FK Unsri for the 2024 period, has demonstrated his active involvement in organizing activities within the medical faculty. His experience in participating in social initiatives reflects his dedication to applying his knowledge for the greater good.

Putri Salsabillah is an active student at the Faculty of Medicine, Sriwijaya University (FK Unsri). Putri shows high dedication to the world of education and organizations. In addition to focusing on medical studies, Putri is also actively involved in various organizations on campus. Putri joined the Student Executive Board (BEM) FK Unsri, BPPM Asy-Syifa FK Unsri and IKMB Unsri, where she contributed to various programs aimed at improving the quality of student life and facilitating self-development activities. The balance between lectures and organizational activities is proof that Putri has a high spirit in pursuing achievements and expanding her horizons.

Dyah Fatha Istiqomah, a medical student at the Faculty of Medicine, University of Sriwijaya, who is not only active in academics but also plays a role in various organizations and volunteer activities. She is a member of the Student Executive Board of the Faculty of Medicine, University of Sriwijaya, as the treasurer of the Advocacy and Student Welfare Department, a department that focuses on internal and external student problems, where she excels in managing and administering finances, especially in that department. This also shows her contribution and concern for the sustainability of the lectures of the Faculty of Medicine, University of Sriwijaya students, and shows her dedication to improving lectures in the future. Her membership in the Sriwijaya Medical Assistance Team organization shows her broader devotion to the community regarding health issues. Writing, reading, and drawing are not only hobbies for Dyah but also part of her stages to develop and express her ideas.

Nabila Az-zahra Hasibuan, a student who is active in student activities, by joining the Student Executive Board (BEM) FK Unsri and the Sriwijaya Medical Assistance Team (TBM), shows her commitment to self-development and community service. In addition, she has also been involved in a publication entitled "The Potential of Zinc Oxide Metal Nanoparticle Technology (NP-ZnO) on Anti-TB Drugs as the Latest Modality for the Treatment of Multidrug-Resistant Tuberculosis (MDR-TB)", which shows her interest in academics and research in the health sector.

M. Aditya Nugraha, is a student of FK UNSRI who is active in academics and research. He has published a journal entitled "The Role of Implementing the HPV Vaccination Program with Optimization of Cervical Cancer Screening and Treatment as an Ambitious Strategy to Reduce the Prevalence of Cervical Cancer in Developing Countries: A Literature Review" with his team. In addition, he and his team won a gold medal in the IICYMS competition through a journal entitled "trusT-B: Integrative, Educative, and Assistive e-Health Application as A Preventive Strategy on The Rise of Suspect and Patient of TBC to Achieve SDG's 30". Aditya was also a finalist in the Lupus Olympiad organized by the Indonesian Rheumatology Association in 2024 and a finalist in the RMO Neuropsychiatry competition in the same year, showing his dedication to the fields of medicine and health innovation.

Raisa Qonita, is a medical student at the Faculty of Medicine, University of Surabaya who has achieved scientific achievements, as evidenced by her Gold Medal achievements at international events such as the International Young Moslem Inventors Awards (IYMIA), the International Invention Competition for Young Moslem Scientists (IICYMS) and the Global Youth Invention Competition (GYIC), as well as 3rd Place in Scientific Poster at SPECTRUM 2023 at the faculty level. In addition, Raisa is also actively involved in community service through various Social Service activities, demonstrating her dedication and concern. Her organizational skills are evident from her important role as the General Treasurer of the Faculty of Medicine, University of Surabaya 2023/2024 and Deputy Head of the Information and Communication Department of the Student Executive Board of the Faculty of Medicine, University of Surabaya. Through this position, Raisa demonstrates her skills in financial management and communication, which support the success of the organization.

Nafilah Ramadhanti, a medical student at Universitas Sriwijaya, is highly dedicated to academic pursuits. She actively participates in writing competitions and scientific research, focusing on solutions to health challenges in Indonesia. In addition to her academic contributions, Nafilah is also involved in various organizations, such as the Forum Kajian Ilmiah dan Akademik FK Unsri, AMSA-Unsri, and BEM KM FK Unsri, expanding her contributions in the fields of medicine and health.

www.ingramcontent.com/pod-product-compliance
Lightning Source LLC
Chambersburg PA
CBHW051831250726
48659CB00005B/1791